The Fannie Farmer Junior Cookbook

The Fannie Farmer Junior Cookbook

by Joan Scobey
Illustrated by Patience Brewster

Little, Brown and Company
Boston New York London

New and Revised Paperback Edition

Library of Congress Cataloging-in-Publication Data

Scobey, Joan.
    The Fannie Farmer junior cookbook / by Joan Scobey; illustrated by Patience Brewster. — New and rev. ed.
        p.   cm.
    Includes index.
    Summary: Introduces the basic ingredients, utensils and equipment, and safety aspects of cooking and provides recipes for soups, main dishes, vegetables, and other foods.
    ISBN 0-316-77624-6 (hc)
    ISBN 0-316-77617-3 (pb)
    1. Cookery — Juvenile literature. [1. Cookery.] I. Brewster, Patience, ill. II. Farmer, Fannie Merritt, 1857–1915. III. Title.
TX652.5.S36   1993
641.5 — dc20

10 9 8 7 6 5 4 3 (hc)
10 9 8 7 6 5 4 3 2 1 (pb)

RRD-OH
Printed in the United States of America

Preface

The world of food has changed dramatically since Fannie Farmer brought a new vision to the teaching of cooking. In fact, it has even changed since the last edition of this cookbook in 1957. For one thing, we have new tools and techniques that make the preparation and cooking of food astonishingly quick and easy. We also have new products — fresh, frozen, and packaged — that make cooking a constantly evolving adventure.

Our attitudes are very different, too. We prefer fresh foods to canned. We care about healthy, low-fat foods — without sacrificing any of the good taste, of course. And speaking of taste, we've become very international. We're just as familiar with sushi and guacamole as we are with New England baked beans.

No wonder that more and more of you — boys as well as girls — want to know how to cook. You'll find the essentials here, because good cooking is still grounded in basic principles. You'll find many of the old original recipes, rewritten for new products and equipment available today. You'll also find new recipes for some of your favorite dishes, chosen for your contemporary life-style of sleepovers and school lunches, as well as schedules crowded by after-school activities and community commitments. And because many of you are sometimes in charge of the family dinner, you'll also find information on how to plan a well-balanced meal.

After you master the basic principles, I hope you'll add your own twists to favorite recipes. Trust yourself — don't cook only by the book. And, as Fannie Farmer would surely urge, have fun doing it.

Joan Scobey

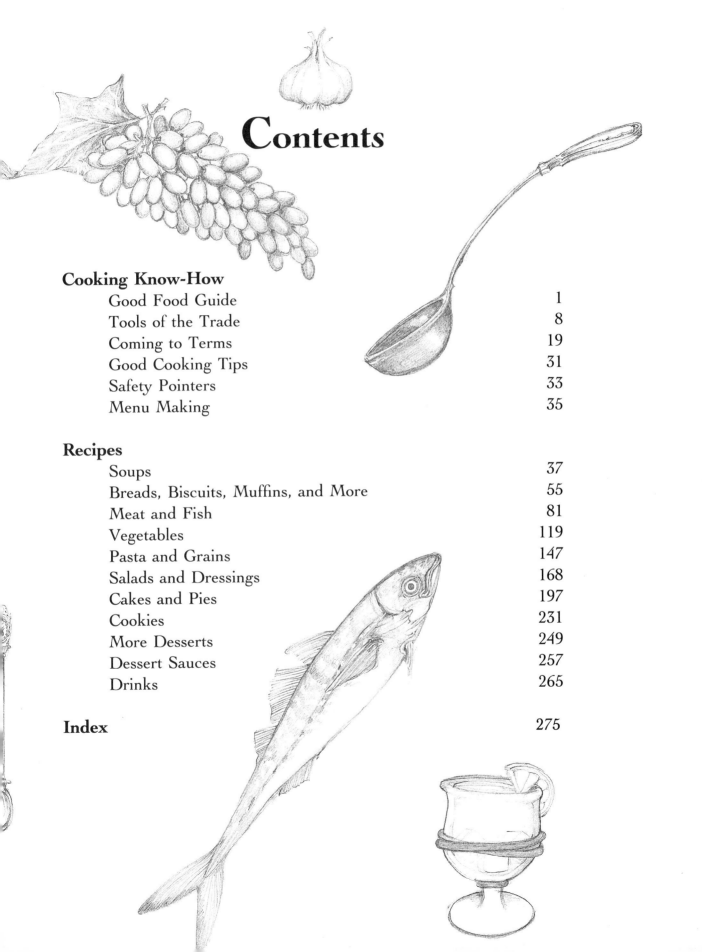

Contents

GOAT CHEESE
Corn Starch
PURE
THICKENING POWDER
Baking Soda

Cooking Know~How
Good Food Guide

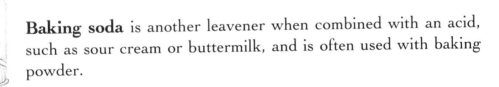

If you haven't had much experience buying food, you may be surprised by the great variety now available even in neighborhood markets: rice from India, oranges from Israel, goat cheese from Italy. As you wander around your local market, you're likely to find unfamiliar fruits, vegetables, and greens, as well as new products you'll want to try. That's the fun of cooking — and it all starts in the food market.

Here's a guide to some basic foods and how to use them.

Baking powder is used to lighten some doughs and batters, often in combination with baking soda. The kind to use is called "double-acting."

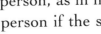

Baking soda is another leavener when combined with an acid, such as sour cream or buttermilk, and is often used with baking powder.

Beef. Because we want to eat healthier foods, especially with less cholesterol, beef is now younger and less fatty than it was in former years. When you buy beef, check for ruddy meat and clear white fat; steaks and roasts should have thin veins of fat, called marbling. For hamburgers, look for bright red meat and minimal fat (less than 18 to 20 percent, if it is listed on the label). You can easily grind your own in a food processor from chunks of chuck and/or round. Figure on ¼ to ⅓ pound of boneless beef per person, as in hamburger or minute steaks, and twice as much per person if the steak or roast has a bone.

1

Bread crumbs. Fresh bread crumbs are easy to make and much tastier than the store-bought packaged variety. Put slices or crusts of fresh bread in a food processor and process until they are well pulverized. White bread is most commonly used, but rye and whole-wheat breads can also be processed, and they have nice snappy flavors. Store them in the freezer in an airtight plastic bag.

Butter is labeled *lightly salted* or *sweet,* which means unsalted. Many professionals prefer sweet butter for baking, but the difference is marginal, so use whichever you prefer. Butter stored in the freezer keeps for months and can be defrosted and refrozen. In the refrigerator it lasts about a week or two, and should be tightly wrapped.

Chicken is labeled according to age, from young broilers or fryers (they mean the same thing) to older and larger roasters and mature hens for stewing. The color of the skin doesn't matter, but chicken should be moist and plump with a fresh odor. Allow about ¾ to 1 pound per person for birds with bones, ⅓ pound per person for boneless breasts. Rinse chicken in cold water as soon as you get home, wrap it loosely, and refrigerate it for no more than a day or two. After preparing it, wash your hands, knives, and cutting board in hot soapy water to prevent contamination. (See **A Special Warning,** page 33.)

Chocolate for cooking is *unsweetened, semisweet,* or *sweet* and usually comes in scored bars or in individually wrapped 1-ounce squares. Chocolate bits or chips are semisweet and are commonly available in 6- and 12-ounce packages; bits or chips are interchangeable with semisweet squares.

Cornstarch is a powder used as a thickening agent and must be dissolved in a small amount of cold water before being added to hot sauces. It's often used in Chinese cooking to produce the characteristic thick, shiny sauces.

Cream for whipping has at least 30 percent fat content and is called *heavy cream.* Light cream and half-and-half don't have enough fat for whipping and are used primarily for sauces and coffee.

Eggs are graded according to their size. These recipes (and most cookbooks) use the size labeled *large* (which is actually not as big as *extra large* and *jumbo*). It doesn't matter if the eggs are white or brown — they taste the same — but discard any raw egg that is cracked.

Fish. Buy fish that's as fresh as possible. Look for bright eyes, shiny skin that springs back when you press it, and a clean sea aroma; avoid any fish that looks dull and gummy and has a strong fishy smell. Choose fish that's refrigerated on ice, not already packaged. You can buy fish whole, just as it is caught, or dressed and ready for cooking, which means scaled and eviscerated, with the head, tail, and fins removed. Dressed fish is also sold as steaks, which are cross-section slices of large fish that include the backbone, and fillets, which are the boneless sides cut lengthwise. Figure about ¾ to 1 pound of whole fish per person, ½ pound per person of dressed fish, steaks, or fillets. Refrigerate the fish immediately and use it within a day or two.

Flour is a fine meal from an edible grain, most commonly wheat, that is ground either by machine or between millstones (when it's described as *stone-ground*). *Gluten* is a protein in flour that has the capacity to become elastic and expand, which makes dough rise, develops flavor, and eventually produces a sturdy, springy bread. Flours differ in their gluten content and in the ways they are best used. In these recipes flour means all-purpose unless otherwise designated.

> **All-purpose flour** is made from hard winter wheat and soft spring wheat and has a moderate gluten content.
> **Cake flour** is finely milled from soft wheat and has a low gluten content.

Self-rising flour, either all-purpose or cake, contains baking powder and salt.

Whole-wheat flour is milled from the whole grain; it has a nutty flavor, a lot of nutrients, and a high gluten content.

Rye flour, made from rye grain, has a high gluten content that doesn't have much elasticity, so it is usually combined with all-purpose flour.

Cornmeal is not a true flour but a coarse meal made from corn; it has no gluten at all, so it's always combined with all-purpose flour for corn bread.

Ham. Most hams you'll find in your neighborhood market will be cured and smoked, and sold either partially or fully cooked. Even ready-to-eat hams improve on being heated through, whether or not they are also glazed. Buy a whole ham with the bone in (it loses flavor when the bone is removed); or buy half hams — the butt end has more meat and the shank end more flavor. Picnic ham is smoked pork shoulder. Figure about ½ pound per person.

Lamb comes from sheep less than a year old (it's called mutton when it is from older sheep, and it's not often seen in the United States). For roasting you can use the whole leg, with the bone in, or buy a half leg — the butt end is meatier than the shank end. You can broil a boned and flattened (called *butterflied*) leg of lamb, or broil or panfry chops cut from the rib or the loin. Figure about ½ pound per person.

Margarine is a vegetable fat, primarily useful as a low-cholesterol alternative to butter as a spread. Although it doesn't have the good taste of butter, you can substitute it for butter in baking, if necessary, but never use it for frying or sautéing because it burns easily.

Oils. There are various kinds of oils, pressed from different seeds, fruits, and nuts, such as olives, corn, peanuts, safflowers, and soybeans. Store them in a cool cupboard, not in the refrigerator.

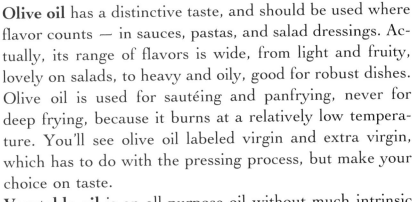

Olive oil has a distinctive taste, and should be used where flavor counts — in sauces, pastas, and salad dressings. Actually, its range of flavors is wide, from light and fruity, lovely on salads, to heavy and oily, good for robust dishes. Olive oil is used for sautéing and panfrying, never for deep frying, because it burns at a relatively low temperature. You'll see olive oil labeled virgin and extra virgin, which has to do with the pressing process, but make your choice on taste.

Vegetable oil is an all-purpose oil without much intrinsic flavor. It is useful for cooking because it withstands high heat. Many oils, among them corn, peanut, safflower, and soybean, can be used interchangeably.

Walnut oil is a special delicacy, to be saved for salad dressings.

Pepper. Peppercorns ground in a mill have more freshness and zest than packaged ground pepper.

Pork. Pork can be found in many cuts. A leg or loin can be used for roasting, and chops should be baked or braised, rather than broiled, to keep them moist. The trick is to cook pork long enough to kill any of the parasites that can cause trichinosis (generally to an internal temperature of about 160°F.) but not so long that it dries out and gets stringy. Buy meat that is pinkish, with white fat, and allow ⅓ to ½ pound per person.

Salad greens. See **Salads and Dressings,** page 168.

Sugars and sweeteners. In baking recipes different kinds of sugars are not interchangeable, either in kind or in amount. Nor can you substitute liquid sweeteners and syrups for dry sugars. Each kind has its own sweetness factor and properties and sometimes a distinctive flavor.

5

Granulated sugar, the ordinary table sugar, is called for in these recipes unless another kind is specified.

Superfine sugar is finely ground granulated sugar, often used in drinks and desserts.

Confectioners' sugar, sometimes called *powdered sugar,* is very fine granulated sugar with cornstarch added to make it powdery. It is used mainly for frostings and to dust the top of cakes.

Brown sugar comes as light or dark, depending on the amount of molasses added to it. Dark brown has a richer taste, light brown is more commonly used in baking; if a recipe doesn't specify which one, you can use either. Store them in tightly capped containers. If the sugar hardens, add a few drops of water and warm it in a very slow oven (250°F.) for 15 minutes. Granulated brown sugar (sometimes called Brownulated) pours easily but is unpredictable in cooking.

Molasses is the residue after granulated sugar has been processed from sugarcane. It comes as dark or light, and it should be unsulfured. Sulfured molasses and blackstrap molasses have unpleasant flavors.

Corn syrup also comes as light or dark; the dark is much sweeter.

Maple syrup is the reduced sap of the maple tree.

Honey, made by bees, is sweeter than table sugar and a delicious spread. It may vary in flavor depending upon the flowers the bees collected nectar from.

Veal is the meat from young calves, tender, virtually fat-free, and very expensive. To keep the meat moist, thin slices or scallops, cutlets, and chops are best cooked by sautéing, panfrying, and braising; roasts are either braised or well basted. Allow about ⅓ pound per person for boneless cuts and at least ½ pound per person for roasts with bones.

Vegetable shortening, a creamy white solid with little or no taste made from vegetable oils, makes tender and flaky pie crusts and can withstand the high heat of frying. It comes in a can, doesn't need refrigeration, and has an almost indefinite shelf life.

Vinegar always has a sharp acidic edge, but some types are milder than others. **Distilled white vinegar** and **cider vinegar** are very sharp and generally are used for pickling. **Red and white wine vinegars** are milder and appropriate for salads. You can turn a wine vinegar into an **herb vinegar** by steeping a few sprigs of an herb in the bottle for several weeks (dill, basil, and tarragon make lovely herb vinegars). **Fruit vinegars** are made the same way; raspberry and red currant vinegar are popular. **Balsamic vinegar** is an Italian vinegar aged in vats that give it a rich, mellow flavor. Other special vinegars include **Japanese rice vinegar,** with a light, fresh taste, and **Spanish sherry vinegar,** with a nutty flavor.

Yeast, the most common leavening agent in breads, needs sugar, starch, and liquid to become active. The easiest way to buy it is in the dry granular form that comes in ¼-ounce foil packages with a shelf life of several months.

Note: When you buy packaged foods, stop to read the labels. The ingredients are listed in order of decreasing quantity, although the specific amount may not be given. For instance, you'll see whether a can of chicken stock contains salt and how high up in the list it appears, so that if you use it in a sauce, you'll be careful about adding more salt; or if a cake flour already contains baking powder, you won't add any more.

Tools of the Trade

Cooking is easier and more successful when you use the right implements. If you've ever been to a kitchen store, you know there are a lot of gadgets on the market and many specialized appliances. Not all of them are necessary or even particularly useful. Even among the basic pots and pans, there is a large variety of sizes and shapes. Here's a checklist of the basic tools you will need for cooking.

Small Appliances

Electric mixer. A heavy-duty model with a whip for beating egg whites, a paddle for all-purpose mixing, and a dough hook for bread making is the most useful. Two bowls are handy.

Electric hand mixer. This is light and portable, useful for frostings and small jobs, such as whipping a little cream.

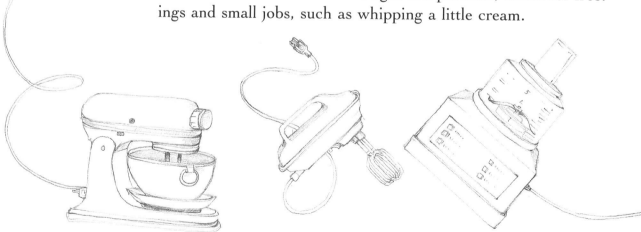

Food processor. This takes the work out of slicing, chopping, grating, pureeing, and shredding with a variety of blades and disks. One of the few things it doesn't do well is whip egg whites or cream.

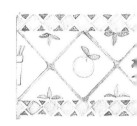

Microwave. Microwave ovens come in different sizes and wattages, and a large microwave, 550 to 700 watts, cooks more quickly and efficiently than a smaller, lower-wattage model. You can also put a larger plate or platter inside, enabling you to cook more food at one time.

If your microwave doesn't have a built-in turntable or if the oven isn't built to rotate the waves, buy a separate turntable so you won't have to turn the food yourself halfway through the cooking.

Pots, Pans, Casseroles, and Baking Dishes

Teakettle. It doesn't matter what it's made of, but it should hold 2 quarts of water. A whistle that lets you know when the water is boiling is handy.

Double boiler. This is excellent for cooking custards and sauces and for reheating cooked foods without danger of burning or overcooking them. Keep the water in the lower part below the bottom of the inset (top pan) so that the food in the top is always over, not in, the boiling water. An inset that holds 3 quarts is the most useful. Stainless steel is best. Try to avoid aluminum, which will discolor sauces containing certain ingredients.

Heavy saucepans with tight-fitting lids. Heavy, flat-bottomed, straight-sided saucepans cook most evenly, and are most useful with tight-fitting covers. Enameled cast-iron or stainless-steel pots are equally good and come in several sizes.

9

8- to 10-quart pot with tight-fitting lid. This is for boiling and blanching foods and making some soups. It should be made of lightweight material (such as aluminum) because a potful of water is heavy. The most useful ones come with two insets: a 3- to 4-inch-deep steamer that rests on the rim; and a deep perforated strainer that fits closely inside the outer pot, providing a safe and easy way of lifting and draining hot foods.

Steamer. A compact, collapsible steamer basket that sits on three legs and fits into many saucepans is useful for steaming small amounts of food.

Skillets with tight-fitting lids. Skillets, or frying pans (they are the same thing), should be heavy, with flat bottoms and a smooth surface. Sloping sides make it easier to lift out such foods as omelets with a pancake turner or broad spatula. Heavyweight aluminum with a nonstick lining and black cast iron are both good. The most useful sizes are 8- and 12-inch pans.

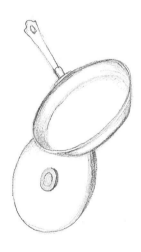

10-inch sauté pan with tight-fitting lid. This has straight 2¼-inch sides, and is made of unlined heavy-duty cast aluminum.

Enameled cast-iron casseroles with tight-fitting covers. These are useful and attractive casseroles; they can be used on top of the stove or in the oven and then go right to the table. The most useful sizes are the 2- or 3-quart, and the 5- or 6-quart. If you are making large quantities, you may want a 7- or even 9-quart oval.

Roasting pan with rack. A heavy metal pan about 16 × 11 inches, with its own rack that rests on the top edge, is good for most roasting and broiling tasks and can also serve as a water bath for small baking cups that must sit in boiling water.

Collapsible V-shaped rack. This fits in the bottom of a roasting pan and holds poultry and roasts while they cook.

 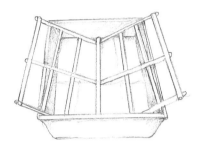

Casseroles, or bake-and-serve dishes. A multipurpose collection includes an 8- or 9-inch round and a 9 × 13-inch rectangle. They are most useful if they are microwave-safe and pretty enough to go to the table.

Microwave containers. Glass, ceramics, plastics, and paper goods that are marked "microwave-safe" are the main materials to use in a microwave oven. Because of the nature of the actual microwaves, you can't use metal of any kind, not even the thin wire that's hidden in the center of bag twists or a plate with a metal rim or decoration.

Containers must fit the inside of the oven. Since the cooking area of each model is a little different, it is helpful to know the interior measurements of your microwave. For large microwave ovens, a dish about 11 × 14 × 2 inches with rounded corners makes maximum use of the space. Any glass or ceramic container can be used for cooking — casseroles, custard cups, dinner plates, soup bowls, coffee mugs, measuring cups, plastic bags, paper plates — so you probably won't need to buy anything to cook with in the microwave.

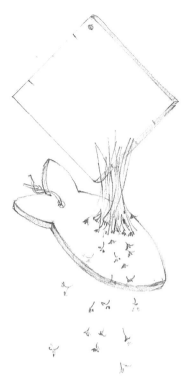

For Cutting, Chopping, and Other Food Preparation

Cutting board. Polyethylene is a relatively new material and excellent for cutting because it doesn't chip or retain odors, and it's easy to clean with soap and water. A large size, about 16 × 20 inches, is most useful. You should have two cutting boards, one for meat and poultry and one for fruits and vegetables (see **Safety Pointers,** page 33).

Knives. The knives you'll use most frequently are a small paring knife, about 3 inches long; a medium-sized utility knife, about 5 or 6 inches long; an 8- or 9-inch chef's (or cook's) knife; a bread knife with a serrated edge; and a slicing or carving knife. Keep them in a slotted wooden knife holder rather than loose in a drawer, where they could be a hazard. (Good sets of stainless-steel knives in wooden holders are available at reasonable prices.)

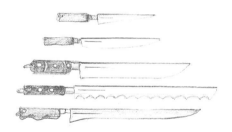

Standing four-sided grater. Each side has different-sized holes, from fine to coarse, and will do practically any grating job you need.

Swivel-bladed vegetable peeler. You'll use this all the time for peeling fruits and potatoes as well as vegetables.

Rotary hand beater. This does a fine job of beating egg whites and whipping cream, especially for small amounts when you don't want to set up the electric mixer.

12

For Baking

Cake Pans. A basic assortment of cake pans includes two 8- or 9-inch rounds, 1½ inches deep; an 8- or 9-inch square pan; a 9 × 13-inch rectangular pan; a 10-inch tube pan.

Loaf pans. You'll need two, about 9 × 5 × 3 inches.

Muffin tins with nonstick linings. You'll need two tins to make 24 muffins at a time. Standard-sized tins have 12 cups about 2½ inches across. A set of smaller tins, with cups about 1½ inches across, makes nice mini-muffins.

Cookie sheets with nonstick linings. These have slightly turned-up ends and rimless sides, and you'll need at least two, if not three, for a batch of cookies.

Jelly-roll pan. This has a 1-inch rim around all four sides and can be used for cookies and other flat baked confections as well as jelly rolls.

Pie pans. A 9-inch pan is a good all-purpose size. Use a dull-finish aluminum pan for pastry crusts and a glass pan for crumb crusts.

Ovenproof glass cups. The most common size holds 6 ounces, perfect for baked custards and puddings, and the 10-ounce version makes nice individual soufflés. Glass cups are also handy for holding measured ingredients when you're cooking and for storing small amounts of leftovers. Keep at least four or six of each size around.

Cake rack. A wire rack lets air circulate around cakes and cookies while they cool. It also doubles as a broiling rack. You'll probably need two of them.

Cake tester. This is a long thin rigid wire you insert into cakes and breads to see if they have finished baking.

Sifter. The spring-action sifter is easy to use for flour alone or to sift together dry ingredients, such as flour, sugar, baking powder, and baking soda.

Pastry blender. Metal wires attached to a handle make easy work of cutting butter or shortening into flour.

Rolling pin. Whether it's one-piece or revolves between its handles, a rolling pin should be heavy to roll dough out well.

Pastry board. You can roll dough out on almost any flat surface, such as a Formica countertop or marble slab, but cleanup is easier if you have a wooden or polyethylene board you can take to the sink. A good size is at least 20 × 24 inches.

Cookie cutters. These are usually 2 to 3 inches in diameter, but you can just as easily cut out rounds of dough with the rim of a glass.

Paper baking cups. These are set into muffin tins, making muffins easily portable and cleanup simple. They are also available with foil outer cups; these can stand alone on a cookie sheet and eliminate the need for a muffin tin.

Ruler. You'll use it primarily for measuring the diameter of rolled-out pastry dough.

Instant meat thermometer. This is smaller, more expensive, and more accurate than the common meat thermometer that stays in the meat during cooking. You never leave this one in the oven, but periodically insert its narrow shaft anywhere in the meat to get an almost instant reading.

Bulb baster. This is what you use to baste a roast in the oven and suck up grease from pan drippings.

Oven mitts. Mitts are safer than pot holders because there's no chance a finger could touch anything hot.

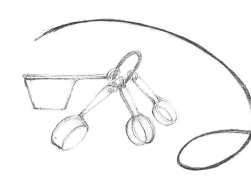

Miscellaneous

Measuring cups. You'll need two sets of measuring cups, one for dry ingredients and another for liquids.

Measuring cups for dry ingredients usually come in sets of four — 1 cup, ½ cup, ⅓ cup, and ¼ cup. The 1-cup measure is marked on one side in ¼-cup increments, and on the other in ⅓-cup fractions.

Measuring cups for wet ingredients are usually made of glass and have a spout and handle for easy pouring. The most useful sizes are 1 cup, 2 cup, and 4 cup. They are all marked in ounces and fractions of cups, and sometimes also in liters.

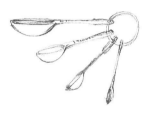

Measuring spoons. A standard set of four includes 1 tablespoon, 1 teaspoon, ½ teaspoon, and ¼ teaspoon.

Mixing bowls. You'll need a set of three in graduated sizes, preferably stainless steel or heavy heatproof glass.

Colander. A large metal one is a staple, useful for draining hot food, such as vegetables and pasta, and rinsing fresh foods.

Hand strainers or sieves. You'll need two sizes, including a small one.

Two-pronged fork. This should be metal, with long tines and a long handle for reaching into a hot oven or deep pot.

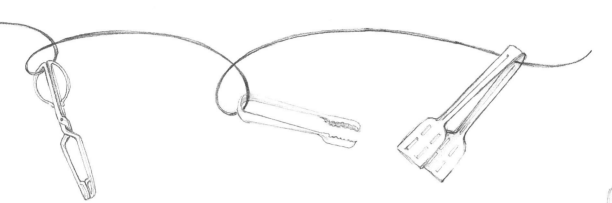

Tongs. Short tongs with smooth ends are useful for turning food in frying pans and skillets; longer tongs are useful for reaching into a hot oven to turn meat or poultry and for taking food out of boiling water.

Spoons. You'll need a variety of long-handled large spoons, both slotted and unslotted, for cooking and mixing. Metal or heavy-duty plastic is good for some jobs, and wooden spoons are good for others.

Spatulas. Rubber spatulas, both wide and narrow, are essential for mixing and for scraping out bowls. Narrow flat metal spatulas are used in baking to apply icings and to free foods from baking pans. Large flat spatulas, both slotted and unslotted, are needed to turn and lift food.

Ladle. This is indispensable for soups, stocks, and sauces.

Wire whisks. Small- and medium-sized wire whisks or whips are handy for all kinds of mixing, stirring, and beating.

Salad spinner. Easiest to use is a plastic unit with an outer container that catches the water from a spinning inner basket.

Pastry brush. You'll use this for basting, glazing, buttering, and many other jobs.

Vegetable brush. Sturdier than a pastry brush, this is good for scrubbing vegetables and potatoes.

Pepper grinder. There's no other way to grind fresh pepper.

Garlic press.

Nutmeg grater.

Hand juicer. You'll need it for squeezing lemons, oranges, and limes for cooking.

Heavy-duty aluminum foil.

Paper towels.

Waxed paper.

Plastic wrap.

String.

Scissors. An all-purpose pair of kitchen shears comes in handy all the time.

Empty coffee can with plastic lid. Keep this in the refrigerator for discarded fat and oil.

Don't worry if you don't have all this equipment. You can blend pastry with two knives, dry salad between layers of paper towels, let cake cool on any rack, sift flour through a sieve rather than a sifter, and improvise in many ways. The only time it's important to use the specified pan is when you're baking.

Coming to Terms

As you make these recipes, you'll come across some instructions that may look odd. For instance, terms like "dust," "seed," and "whip" have different meanings in cooking from those that they have outside the kitchen. Here is a cook's dictionary of definitions and techniques, how to do things and why, and some basic kitchen talk.

Baking means cooking in the oven in dry heat, and usually refers to cakes, cookies, breads, custards, and pudding (it's called roasting when you're cooking meat this way). Don't bake cakes or cookies at the same time as watery foods like custards or soft puddings because those give off steam that may make cakes and cookies too moist. Whatever you bake, leave plenty of room in the oven around each pan. If you're using two racks in the oven, don't place pans directly under each other, but stagger them for maximum heat circulation.

Basting keeps foods moist during cooking. The method is to spoon or paint on a liquid — usually the sauce used in the cooking, pan drippings, a marinade, or melted butter — to add more flavor and to keep the food from drying out. Use a bulb baster, a spoon, or a brush.

Beating is a method of vigorously mixing an ingredient, like whole eggs or egg yolks or a cake batter, to incorporate air. An electric mixer does the job easily, but be careful not to overbeat, for that may make the mixture dry and heavy. To beat by hand, use a whisk or a wooden spoon and turn the mixture over and over briskly in a circular motion that brings the bottom part to the top.

19

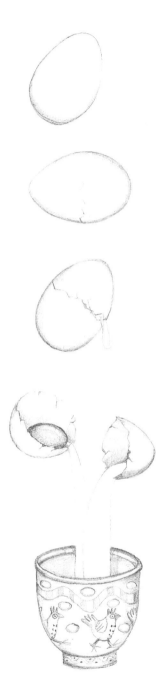

Beating Eggs. Eggs should be at room temperature, not icy cold, so take them from the refrigerator half an hour ahead of time and break them into a bowl. If you are beating the whites and the yolks separately, have two bowls ready and put the whites in one and the yolks in the other.

To **separate the yolk and white of an egg,** tap the egg lightly with a knife or against the edge of a small custard cup, just enough to crack the shell. Hold the egg over the cup with both hands and open the crack a little, letting the white flow out into the cup. Now you can safely widen the crack until the shell splits into two halves; the yolk should be unbroken and resting in one of the halves. If there is any white left in either half of the shell, pour the yolk back and forth from one half to the other, letting the white drip between them into the cup. It's important to keep the white clear of any bits of yolk (the fat in the yolk prevents the white from beating up well), but it won't matter if there is a little white left around the yolk. Drop the yolk from the shell into one bowl and pour the white from the cup into the other before you separate another egg. If the yolk breaks into the white, put the egg, tightly covered, in the refrigerator and use it for another purpose.

Beat whole eggs or egg yolks with a rotary hand beater or an electric mixer. **Beating egg whites** is a little trickier because you want to incorporate as much air as you can in the whites before they get overbeaten and start to lose air. Use a clean dry bowl and beaters. With an electric mixer, start out on slow speed and beat until the whites are foamy. Then increase the speed to medium and beat the whites as much as the recipe says. Many recipes ask you to "beat until the whites are stiff but not dry." That point is reached when the whites stand up in firm glossy peaks when you lift out the beater. Always beat egg whites just before you need them because they lose their volume quickly.

20

To add beaten egg whites to another mixture without losing their airiness, you must combine them very gently, which is often called "folding in." See **Folding in,** page 24.

Blanching means boiling food quickly in water, usually to make it easier to peel or skin it, as with almonds or tomatoes, or to remove excess salt.

Boiling is usually confused with simmering (see **Simmering,** page 29). In a true, or rolling, boil the surface of a heated liquid is bubbling vigorously and continuously. Boiling is used to reduce liquids (see **Reducing,** page 28) and occasionally to cook some vegetables and shellfish, but the action is too strong for most other foods. To bring to a boil means to heat a liquid, often water or soup or stock, over high heat just until bubbles appear on the surface.

Braising is slow, moist-heat cooking in a small amount of liquid, either in the oven or on top of the stove. Common liquids include stock, tomato juice, wine, and well-seasoned water. Good foods for braising are meats, poultry, fish steaks, and some vegetables.

Broiling is cooking under very high heat, so it's important to preheat the broiler for about 15 minutes. Place foods so the top is at least 2 inches away from the source of heat, unless a recipe specifies otherwise. Remember to account for the height of the broiling pan when you set the oven racks in place. For even cooking, let food come to room temperature first.

Browning meat seals in the juices and gives food a nice dark color. It's often the first step in a longer cooking process, which can be in the oven, under the broiler, or on the top of the stove in a skillet. Searing (see **Searing,** page 29) is another way of sealing in juices.

Buttering a baking dish, cookie sheet, or other baking utensil means spreading the required amount of butter or shortening over the bottom and sides of the utensil.

Chill a bowl by setting it into another, larger bowl filled with ice cubes; a stainless-steel smaller bowl works best. If you want to chill food rapidly, use this same setup and put the food in the top bowl, or put it in the freezer for a short time.

Creaming usually refers to combining butter and sugar. Take the required amount of butter out of the refrigerator about an hour ahead so that it will be soft enough to work. Put it into a bowl and beat it with a wooden spoon until it is fluffy. Then add the sugar little by little, rubbing the two together against the side of the bowl with the back of the spoon until they are completely blended, smooth, and fluffy. Or use an electric mixer, beating the butter first and adding the sugar gradually, beating just enough to keep the mixture light.

Cutting in usually refers to incorporating shortening into flour until it's the consistency of cornmeal. The easiest way to do it is with a pastry blender or two knives, using chopping strokes.

Cutting and chopping. There are different ways to describe how to prepare food, depending on the size and shape you want, and they sometimes use different techniques.

To **slice,** set the food (for example, an onion or potato) on a cutting board; you may have to cut a slice from the bottom so it lies flat. Hold the food carefully, tucking your fingers under, slice straight down, and move your hand back from the knife after each slice.

To **julienne,** which produces thin matchstick strips, first cut the food in ⅛-inch-thick slices as described above, then stack the slices and cut straight down on them at ⅛-inch intervals to create the thin strips.

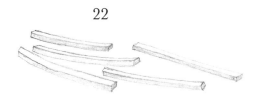

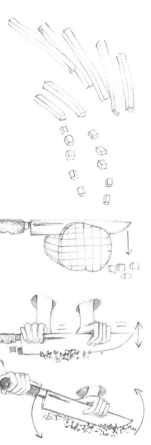

To **dice,** set the food (usually an onion) on a cutting board; you may have to cut a slice from the bottom so it lies flat. First, hold the top, and, starting at the bottom, cut horizontal slices about ⅛ or ¼ inch apart, or whatever size you want your dice. Then, make vertical slices at the same intervals. Last, rotate the cutting board a quarter turn (90 degrees) and hold the food carefully, tucking your fingers under so only your knuckles are near the knife. Cut straight down to create the dice, and move your hand back from the knife after each cut.

To **chop,** hold the top of the blade — not the cutting edge — of a large knife with two hands and bring the knife straight up and down over the food.

To **mince,** first chop the food as described above. Then hold the handle of the knife in one hand and the top of the tip with the other and roll the blade back and forth over the food.

To **cut sticky foods,** such as raisins, dates, or marshmallows, use scissors or a sharp knife, dipped frequently in cold water.

To **cut herbs,** such as parsley or mint, wash them carefully, cut off any heavy stems, and dry them between two paper towels. Put the sprigs in a sturdy glass and snip them with kitchen scissors until they are evenly minced.

Deglazing is a way of enriching pan juices by using the browned particles left in a pan after food has been sautéed or roasted. First take out the food and as much fat as you can (see **Degreasing, page 24**). Then add a little liquid to the pan — it can be stock, cream, even water — and stir with a wooden spoon over moderate heat, scraping and incorporating the particles. The more liquid you add, the less intense the flavor; if you want a stronger flavor, boil down the liquid to concentrate it. Deglazing also makes the pan easier to clean.

Degreasing a hot pan can be tricky. Tilt the pan and draw the fat off with a bulb baster, or skim it off with a wide flat spoon. If you're not using the food right away and plan to reheat it, put it in the refrigerator; the fat will rise to the top, congeal, and is easily removed. This works well for chicken soup, stews, and pot roasts.

Dotting the top means to cut something, usually butter, into small pieces and place them at random over the surface of a food.

Dredging means coating food with another ingredient, usually flour or bread crumbs. You can put the coating on a piece of waxed paper and dip the food in, put it in a paper or plastic bag and shake the food in it, or pour it through a sieve and dust the food over a sheet of waxed paper. Whichever way you choose, shake off the excess coating. Don't flour or crumb the food until you're ready to cook, because the natural moisture in the food will make the coating gummy.

Dust food or a baking pan by lightly sprinkling with a dry ingredient, such as flour, sugar, or cocoa, using a sifter or sieve.

Folding in is a way of adding light airy food, such as whipped cream or beaten egg whites, to a heavier mixture. It's a gentler process than beating, stirring, or mixing because you don't want to lose the airiness. Spoon the lighter mixture over the heavier one. Using a rubber spatula, cut down into the batter and bring the spatula up along the bottom of the bowl, then rotate the bowl a little and repeat the cut-and-fold motion. Continue gently folding and turning until the aerated mixture is evenly distributed.

Frying simply means cooking on top of the stove with fat. **Pan-frying** describes cooking in a skillet on top of the stove with a small amount of fat and is sometimes called sautéing. **Stir-frying** uses just a film of fat and the addition of some liquid. **Deep-fat**

frying requires a deep pot or pan to immerse food completely in very hot fat.

Garnishing is cook talk for decorating a plate or platter with some food that will make the main dish look prettier and complement its taste. Lemon wedges, cherry tomatoes, and sprigs of parsley, mint, or other herbs are common garnishes.

Kneading is working dough with your hands or an electric mixer to bring out the gluten in the flour. See the bread recipes on pages *74–79* for the specific way to do this.

Marinating is immersing foods, usually meat, in an acidic liquid containing some lemon or lime juice, wine, or vinegar that flavors and tenderizes it. The liquid is called a marinade.

Measuring equivalents:
      a pinch = less than ¼ teaspoon
      a dash = a few drops
      3 teaspoons = 1 tablespoon
      2 tablespoons = 1 liquid ounce
      4 tablespoons = ¼ cup
      16 tablespoons = 1 cup
      1 cup = ½ pint
      2 cups = 1 pint (liquid) and 1 pound (dry)
      2 pints = 1 quart
      4 cups = 1 quart or 32 ounces

Measure all ingredients in standard measuring cups and spoons, not just any cup or spoon. Dry ingredients, such as flour, sugar, baking powder, salt, and cinnamon, and liquids, such as water, stock, juice, and oil, are measured in different cups (see **Tools of the Trade,** page 8).

To measure dry ingredients, first stir them and crush any lumps, and sift one or more together, if the recipe calls for that. Dip the appropriate-sized cup or spoon into the ingredient and remove the excess with the edge of a knife, or spoon the dry ingredient into the cup and shake gently to level it. Don't pack down any dry ingredient except brown sugar.

To measure liquids, fill a liquid measuring cup to the level needed, or fill the correct size of measuring spoon to the top.

To measure honey, molasses, or syrups, butter the measuring cup or spoon lightly so the ingredient will pour out more easily. For honey, set the honey jar in a pan of hot water for a few minutes for easier pouring.

To measure a soft fat, such as shortening or soft butter, pack it into a dry measuring cup and level off with a knife or rubber spatula.

Butter and margarine in sticks are easy to measure. One stick is ¼ pound, or 4 ounces, and contains 8 tablespoons, or ½ cup.

Microwaving. A microwave oven cooks food in an entirely different way from traditional methods. It is clean, quick, and doesn't mess up the oven. It also takes a little getting used to. The microwaves move from the outside toward the center, so that food placed on the edge of a container cooks more quickly than food in the center. To get evenly microwaved food, arrange the thickest pieces around the outside and more fragile, less dense food toward the center. For example, lay broccoli florets with their stems pointing out.

Microwaving is superb for steaming and moist-heat cooking, so vegetables and fish are wonderful cooked in a microwave, but it doesn't brown or bake well. You can also cook different foods at the same time, so you can prepare a whole dinner — for instance, fish, vegetables, potatoes — on one plate and take it straight to the table.

The cooking times in these recipes are given for a large

model, and most of the time you'll cook on High, or 100 percent. There are many variables in microwave cooking — the size, amount, and placement of the food, in addition to the size and wattage of the oven — so you may have to adjust cooking times a little. In fact, if you enjoy microwave cooking, a specialized microwave cookbook is a valuable reference.

Two warnings: Don't operate a microwave when it's empty, and always use oven mitts when removing containers, because they can heat up (from the hot food, not the microwaves).

Mixing in simply means to combine ingredients.

Oven temperatures are often described this way:

Very slow	250°F.
Slow	300°F.
Moderately slow	325°F.
Moderate	350°F.
Moderately hot	375°F.
Hot	400°F
Very Hot	450 to 500°F.

Preheat the oven by setting the indicator at the required temperature and turning on the oven. In most ovens a light indicates when the oven has reached the set heat; if your oven doesn't have a light, preheat it for 15 minutes.

Pan-broiling actually means frying without fat and has nothing to do with broiling. The hot skillet is sometimes sprinkled with salt or lightly rubbed with fat from the food, but in general pan-broiling relies on fat released from the cooking food, such as hamburgers or chops.

Parboiling is partially cooking food by boiling, in preparation for further cooking by some other method.

Paring, or **peeling,** is to remove the skin of vegetables and fruits. A vegetable peeler does the job neatly for most of them. For onions and garlic, cut the top off with a knife and peel off the papery skin, using the edge of the knife.

Poaching, unlike simmering, where you bring a cooking liquid to a boil and then turn down the heat, means heating the liquid until it barely bubbles and never comes close to a boil.

Preheating. See **Oven temperatures,** page 27.

Pureeing means to crush food into a smooth mixture, called a puree. The food processor or blender is the most efficient way to do it, but you can also use a food mill.

Reducing a soup or stock or sauce means boiling it at high heat to evaporate some of the liquid, which reduces the quantity and intensifies the flavor.

Roasting means cooking in the oven in dry heat. Practically every kind of meat and fish, as well as many vegetables, can be roasted. It's exactly the same method as baking. For some unexplained reason, when fish and ham are cooked this way, they are called baked fish and baked ham.

Rolling out dough is the process of preparing dough for its intended use, usually very thin for a pie crust or thicker for biscuits. Place a ball of dough on a floured pastry board and with a rolling pin make short quick strokes in every direction so the dough thins out evenly to the specified thickness.

Sautéing is similar to panfrying in that the food is first cooked in a little fat in a skillet; classically, it means that the food is removed and the pan drippings are then used to make a sauce.

Scalding milk is to bring it just to a boil over moderate heat, or until a film starts to form on the surface (the film should be removed).

Searing meat is another way of sealing in juices by cooking at very high heat for a short time.

Seeding means to remove the seeds from a fruit or vegetable, usually a pepper or tomato.

Separating eggs. See **Beating Eggs,** page 20.

Sifting removes lumps from dry ingredients and aerates them slightly. Sift ingredients separately or together through a sifter or sieve into a mixing bowl or onto waxed paper.

Simmering is really what most people mistakenly call boiling. Bring the cooking liquid to a boil over high heat just until bubbles appear on the surface, add the food, then turn the heat down and adjust it so the surface ripples gently.

Steaming is a method of cooking in which food, in a basket or perforated container, is suspended over, but never touches, boiling water. A tight-fitting lid that prevents any steam from escaping is essential. Steaming is a wonderful way of cooking crisp bright vegetables and moist fish.

Stewing is slow, moist-heat cooking in which the food is entirely immersed in a liquid, commonly stock, tomato juice, wine, well-seasoned water, or a combination of them. Stewing can be done either in the oven or on the stove top.

Stirring, or **stirring in,** means using a spoon or whisk in a circular motion to combine ingredients or to make sure that stovetop mixtures are cooking evenly and are not sticking to the bottom of the pot.

Stock is what cooks call clear soup or consommé when it's used for cooking rather than for eating at table.

Turning out means to remove or unmold a cake or other dish from the pan it was baked, cooked, or chilled in, usually by turning it upside down.

Warming plates. Some foods, especially meats, cool rapidly as soon as they are sliced or carved, so serve them on heated plates or platters. Warm them in an oven set on the lowest setting, in the dishwasher on the dry cycle, or on an electric hot tray.

Whipping is a way of combining ingredients and incorporating a little air, using a whip or whisk. Purists make whipped cream with a balloon whip, but it's a lot easier to beat the cream with an electric mixer. Chill the bowl (metal or glass) and the beaters for an hour or two first.

Good Cooking Tips

It seems obvious, but it's important to read through every recipe before you start. You'll get an idea of what's ahead, and what you'll need. If there are any instructions you don't understand, look them up in **Coming to Terms** (page 19). And leave yourself plenty of time. It's hard to tell how long a recipe will take to prepare, especially the first time you make it, but you can count on its not going as fast as you think.

Also get out all the utensils and ingredients that are called for, and if any need special preparation, do it first. For example, grease the baking pans, cut the herbs, chop the vegetables, measure the sugar, sift the flour, melt the butter. All the ingredients should be ready in the form the recipe specifies so once you actually start cooking, you won't have to stop in the middle. That's not just good planning, it's often crucial to the recipe because you may not have time to wait for melted butter to cool or even to butter and flour a pan.

Savvy cooks learn how to avoid unnecessary work, especially when it comes to cleaning up. Here are a few tips:

◆ Don't use more bowls and utensils than you need.

◆ Measure dry ingredients onto waxed paper when you can.

◆ If you're beating both egg whites and yolks, beat the whites first; then, without washing the beater, beat the yolks.

◆ Wash up as you go along whenever you can. The job is much easier if you do it before the food has time to stick or dry. You can often do

31

a little cleanup while waiting for a kettle to boil or for muffins to finish baking.

◆ Before washing, scrape bowls clean with a rubber spatula. If they are sticky, wipe them first with a paper towel.

◆ Rinse the blades of a rotary hand beater in cold water immediately after using, especially after beating egg yolks.

◆ Don't put knives in dish-washing water because the blades are dulled by bumping against other things, and the handles get loose if soaked. Instead, wipe knife blades with a hot soapy dishcloth, rinse under the faucet, and dry right away before the blade gets rusty.

◆ Soaking is good for most dirty dishes and pans except aluminum, which discolors in water.

◆ If some food burns in a pan, fill the pan with cold water, add a tablespoon of baking soda, and heat slowly on top of the stove. Then fill a basin with hot soapy water, add a little ammonia, and wash the pan. You may need steel wool to scrub off the last bits.

Safety Pointers

Sharp knives, hot pots, steaming kettles — these go with the territory, and even experienced cooks are always mindful of them. So here are a few good rules of the road to cook by:

◆ Wash your hands before handling any food.

◆ Don't leave perishable food at room temperature more than two hours, and it's best to refrigerate it even sooner.

◆ Always set pots on a stove top or range so their handles are turned in and don't stick out beyond the stove.

◆ Get in the habit of always using oven mitts when handling hot pots and pans. These include microwave containers.

◆ Microwaved food that has been covered with plastic wrap can be a trap for scalding steam, so carefully poke a hole in the plastic on the side away from you to let out some steam before removing the rest of the plastic.

A Special Warning: You may have heard about "salmonella." It's an organism that is sometimes present in meats, poultry, and raw eggs and is killed by cooking with high heat. You can't see it or smell it, so you must take special precautions when you handle these ingredients raw — but there's no problem after they are cooked.

Here's what to do: Use one cutting board for meat and poultry, and a separate one for fruits and vegetables — and never mix them up. After cutting or handling meats and poultry, wash the cutting board and the knives and other utensils that touched the meat or poultry, as well as your hands, in hot soapy water.

Don't eat raw eggs or use them in any recipe that doesn't require cooking. The risk of salmonella poisoning has grounded some favorite recipes, like chocolate mousse and uncooked cake icings, and, I'm sorry to say, it also means you shouldn't eat raw cake or cookie batter.

Menu Making

You're in charge of making the family dinner, the whole meal, from soup to nuts. First of all, don't panic. The whole idea of what to serve at a meal is now refreshingly different from the traditional meat-vegetables-potato main course, plus starter and dessert. In fact, appetizers and main courses can be practically anything you like.

For example, serve fresh broccoli or asparagus as a starter instead of with the main dish. Add some meat and vegetables to a soup and move it from first course to the main event accompanied by good chewy bread. When summer vegetables are at their flavorful peak, broil or steam a few of your favorite for a delicious, colorful, and very different main course. A well-planned meal needn't be elaborate; in fact, a good motto to remember is, simpler is better.

When you're putting a menu together, choose foods that lend a variety of flavors, textures, and colors to the whole meal. If you start with a creamy white potato soup, don't end with vanilla ice cream. If the main dish is a stew with lots of carrots and onions, don't start with vegetable soup or even vegetables vinaigrette. Chilled carrot soup, not spicy gazpacho, is a good prelude to hot chili. Save sliced tomatoes for a meal that doesn't include pasta with tomato sauce.

When you're actually planning the menu, keep these practical considerations in mind:

◆ Use fresh foods that are at their peak. They taste better, are more economical, and usually require less dressing up (that means less work) than their canned, frozen, or out-of-season counterparts. For example, one of the most delicious ways to start a summer meal is with a plate of thick-sliced vine-ripened tomatoes, topped with snipped fresh basil and drizzled with olive oil.

◆ Check the fridge for leftovers. If you've learned the savvy chef's trick of saving everything — even quarter-cups of last night's vegetables, meats, pastas, rice, whatever — you can turn a soup, an omelet, or a salad into a main course. Or combine leftover meat and vegetables with pasta or rice, and you have another main course.

◆ Try to have at least one course you can make ahead, so you don't have too many last-minute jobs to handle at the same time. It might be vegetables vinaigrette or a salad to start with, or a main course stew, or cookies and fruit for dessert.

◆ If one recipe is a hands-on sauté or stir-fry, for the rest of the meal choose other dishes that you don't have to watch closely. A roast and baked potatoes would fill the bill.

◆ If you're making two or more recipes that need careful monitoring, work out the timing before you start so that different tasks don't come up at the same time. You don't want to whip last-minute egg whites when the sauté pan has to be deglazed.

When you plan a meal you can cook with ease and that's nicely balanced for taste and texture, you should check to see that it's also reasonably balanced nutritionally. Does it have fresh vegetables and fruit (simple carbohydrates)? Bread, pasta, rice (complex carbohydrates)? Some meat or fish (protein)? You won't have to plan for fat, which you'll get in butter, oils, meats, and cheeses. Although one meal doesn't have to reflect complete nutritional needs, a nice balance makes for good and healthful eating.

Now for the recipes — and the fun.

Recipes
Soups

Vegetable Soup

The chicken stock makes this a nice rich soup. You can use other vegetables, such as fresh tomatoes, peas, beans, and corn, as available.

Serves 6

Ingredients
1 large celery stalk with
   leaves
1 large carrot
1 medium turnip
1 potato
1 medium onion
4 tablespoons (½ stick)
   butter
6 cups Chicken Stock (page
   52)
Salt
Freshly ground pepper
2 teaspoons finely cut
   parsley

Equipment
Measuring cup
Measuring spoons
Knife
Mixing bowl
Vegetable peeler
Large saucepan and lid
Wooden spoon

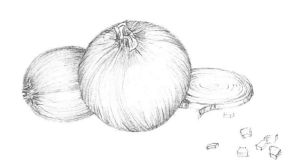

1. Wash all the vegetables. Cut the celery into ¼-inch slices and put them into the mixing bowl. Peel the carrot and cut it into ¼-inch slices; add them to the bowl. Peel the turnip and potato, cut them into ½-inch cubes, and add them to the bowl. Peel and chop the onion and add to the other vegetables.

2. Melt the butter in the large saucepan and add all the vegetables. Cook them for 10 minutes, stirring occasionally with the wooden spoon.

3. Add the chicken stock and bring it to a boil. Partially cover the saucepan with the lid, turn the heat down, and simmer the vegetables about 15 to 20 minutes, or until they are soft.

4. Taste the soup for seasoning and add salt and pepper, if necessary.

5. Just before serving the soup, sprinkle with parsley.

French Onion Soup

For the best flavor, make this soup a day ahead.

Serves 4

Ingredients

2 tablespoons butter
2 medium onions, peeled and
    thinly sliced
1 tablespoon flour
4 cups beef stock
4 slices of French bread, ½
    inch thick
¼ cup freshly grated
    Parmesan cheese

Equipment

Measuring cup
Measuring spoons
Large heavy saucepan with
    lid
Wooden spoon
Oven-proof soup bowls
Ladle
Oven mitts

1. Melt the butter in the saucepan. Add the sliced onions and cook over low heat for 5 minutes, or until the onions are tender, stirring with the wooden spoon. They should be yellow, not brown.

2. Stir in the flour and cook, stirring, 1 minute longer.

3. Pour in the beef stock, bring it to a boil, then lower the heat, partially cover the pan with the lid, and simmer for 30 minutes.

4. If you are making the soup a day ahead, let it cool, then

refrigerate it in the saucepan. When you are ready to use it, heat it thoroughly over medium heat.

5. Preheat the oven to 400°F. and lightly toast the French bread on an oven rack.

6. Set the soup bowls on a cookie sheet or in a shallow pan and place one slice of the toasted bread in each one. Ladle the hot soup over the bread in the bowls and sprinkle with the grated cheese.

7. Wearing oven mitts, carefully set the tray of soup bowls in the oven for a few minutes until the cheese is melted and brown.

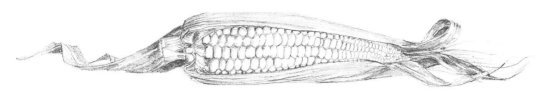

Corn Chowder

This is a great way to use leftover ears of corn, either cooked or raw. Or make this soup anytime with frozen corn kernels.

Serves 6

Ingredients
1½-inch cube of salt pork, cut into small pieces
1 medium onion, peeled and chopped
4 medium potatoes, peeled and cubed
2 cups water
2 cups corn kernels, fresh or frozen
4 cups milk
Salt
Freshly ground pepper
3 tablespoons butter

Equipment
Measuring cups
Large heavy saucepan and lid
Large spoon
Fork

1. Cook the pork slowly in the saucepan until the fat melts and the pork bits are brown. Add the chopped onion and cook 5 minutes, stirring often.

2. Add the potatoes and water to the pan, cover, and cook slowly until the potatoes are tender, testing with a fork every few min-

utes. The smaller the potatoes are cubed, the faster they will be done.

3. Add the corn and the milk and continue cooking another 5 to 10 minutes, until the soup is hot.

4. Taste the soup for seasoning and add salt and pepper, if necessary. Stir in the butter and serve.

Split Pea Soup

This is an easy-to-make, hearty soup for cold weather.

Sreves 6 to 8

Ingredients
1 smoked ham bone or pork
    knuckles (about 1 to 2
    pounds)
2 cups (16 ounces) dried
    split peas
2 medium potatoes, peeled
    and quartered
2 medium onions, peeled,
    then quartered or sliced
8 cups water
Salt
Freshly ground pepper
1 cup Croutons (page 46)

Equipment
Measuring cups
8- to 10-quart pot
Ladle
Food processor or blender
Large pitcher or bowl

1. Put the bone or knuckles, split peas, potatoes, and onions in the pot and cover with 8 cups of water. Bring to a boil and let the soup simmer, uncovered, for 1 hour, or until the peas are soft.

2. Remove the ham bone from the pot and discard it.

3. Ladle a few cupfuls of soup at a time into the blender or processor, process until smooth, then pour it into the pitcher or bowl. Repeat until you have processed all the soup.

4. Pour the soup back into the pot. Taste for seasoning and add salt and pepper, if necessary. Depending on the saltiness of the ham, you may need up to 1 tablespoon salt.

5. Reheat over medium heat and serve garnished with Croutons (page 46).

Croutons

Croutons are small cubes of bread that are sautéed or slowly dried in the oven. They are used in soups and salads and are sprinkled over scrambled eggs. You can buy packaged croutons, but they're not nearly as good as the fresh-flavored ones you make yourself.

Makes 1½ cups

Ingredients
6 slices of day-old white or
    rye bread
4 tablespoons butter

Equipment
Cutting board
Knife
12-inch skillet
Slotted spatula
Paper towels
Slotted spoon

1. Cut the crusts from the bread, then cut the bread into ¼-inch cubes.

2. Melt the butter in the skillet. When the butter begins to sizzle, add the bread cubes and sauté them until they are lightly browned. Turn them with the spatula so they brown evenly on all sides.

3. Lay a double thickness of paper towels on the counter and, using the slotted spoon, remove the browned croutons and spread them out on the paper towels to drain.

If you don't use all the croutons, you can keep them for a week or two in a covered jar in the refrigerator.

Variations

Herbed Croutons: Before sautéing the croutons, add 2 teaspoons of dried herbs or 2 tablespoons of minced fresh herbs to the melted butter. Parsley or tarragon, or a blend of both, makes flavorful croutons.

Garlic Croutons: Substitute 2 tablespoons of olive oil for half the butter and add a peeled, split clove of garlic. When the croutons are browned, drain them on the paper towels and discard the garlic clove.

Gazpacho

This is a refreshing warm-weather soup.

Serves 6

Ingredients
4 ripe tomatoes
2 small cucumbers
1 large onion
1 green pepper
2 ribs celery
2 garlic cloves
4 cups tomato juice
¼ cup olive oil
2 tablespoons red wine
    vinegar
1 tablespoon fresh lemon
    juice
Salt
Freshly ground pepper
1 cup Herbed Croutons
    (page 47)

Equipment
Measuring cups
Measuring spoons
Cutting board
Knife
Large bowl
Large spoon
Ladle
Food processor or blender
Large pitcher or bowl
Plastic wrap

1. Peel, quarter, and seed the tomatoes and put them in the large bowl.

2. Peel the cucumbers and cut in quarters lengthwise. Remove

the seeds with a sharp knife. Cut the cucumbers into 1-inch chunks and put them in the large bowl.

3. Peel the onion, chop it, and add to the large bowl.

4. Cut the green pepper in quarters lengthwise and remove the seeds. Cut into ½-inch pieces and add to the large bowl.

5. Remove the leafy ends of the celery and cut the stalks into ¼-inch slices. Add to the large bowl.

6. Peel the garlic cloves, cut them into quarters, and add to the large bowl.

7. Add the tomato juice, olive oil, wine vinegar, and lemon juice to the vegetables in the bowl and mix with the spoon. Ladle the mixture into a food processor or blender in batches and process until the soup is almost smooth but still has a little texture. As each batch is processed, pour it into the pitcher or another large bowl.

8. Taste for seasoning and add salt and pepper, if necessary. Cover the soup with plastic wrap and refrigerate overnight to let the flavors mellow.

9. Ladle into individual bowls and garnish with Herbed Croutons.

Chilled Carrot Soup

This is a lovely thick, cool, warm-weather soup, easily made in the microwave.

Makes 3 to 4 servings

Ingredients
1 pound (about 5 large) carrots
1 cup boiling water
1 cup Chicken Soup (page 52) or canned broth
1 tablespoon butter or margarine
1 teaspoon salt
¾ cup plain yogurt
1 tablespoon snipped dill

Equipment
Measuring cups
Measuring spoons
Vegetable peeler
Knife
Saucepan with lid or microwave-safe bowl
Plastic wrap
Food processor
Mixing bowl

1. Wash the carrots and scrape them with the vegetable peeler, then slice them about ¼ inch thick.

2. Cook them on the stove or in a microwave: For the stove, put the carrots in the saucepan, add an inch or two of boiling water, cover, and cook for about 10 minutes, until the carrots are tender. For the microwave, put the carrots in the microwave-safe bowl, cover tightly with plastic wrap, and cook on High for about 6 minutes.

3. Drain the carrots and transfer them to the food processor. Add the chicken soup, butter or margarine, and salt and process until the carrots are smooth.

4. Pour the soup into the mixing bowl and stir in the yogurt. Cover with foil or plastic wrap and chill.

5. Serve the chilled soup with a sprinkling of snipped dill.

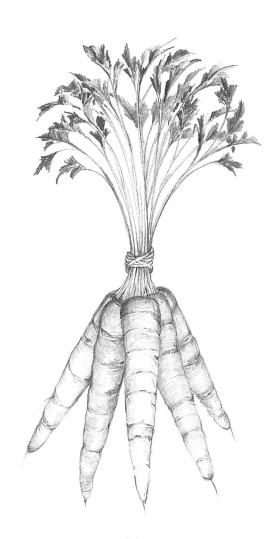

Chicken Soup or Stock

Stock and soup are actually the same item; the difference is generally in how you use it. Served as part of a meal, it's called soup; use it in a recipe and it's called stock.

Makes 6 to 8 cups

Ingredients
10 cups water
1 tablespoon salt
1 large onion
2 carrots
Leafy tops of 3 celery ribs
1 small bunch parsley, or
1 package soup greens
    instead of the onion,
    carrots, celery, and
    parsley
1 bay leaf
½ teaspoon dried thyme
5 whole black peppercorns
1 3- to 4-pound chicken, cut
    into serving pieces and
    washed well

Equipment
Measuring cup
Measuring spoons
Large heavy pot with lid
Vegetable peeler
Knife
2 large mixing bowls
String
Slotted spoon
Large strainer
Large spoon

1. Pour the water into the pot, add the salt, and bring to a boil.

2. Meanwhile, prepare the vegetables and put them in one of the mixing bowls: Peel and quarter the onion; scrape the carrots and cut them into 2-inch pieces; tie the celery tops and parsley together with string.

3. When the water is boiling, carefully add the onion, carrots, celery tops and parsley, bay leaf, thyme, peppercorns, and chicken. When the water comes to a boil again, reduce the heat to low, partially cover the pot, and let the soup simmer for 45 minutes. Remove the lid and simmer, uncovered, 30 minutes more.

4. Remove the chicken pieces and carrots with the slotted spoon and set them aside in the mixing bowl to cool.

5. With the slotted spoon remove and discard the onion, celery tops and parsley, bay leaf, and peppercorns.

6. Taste the stock. If it's too weak, boil it briskly for another 15 minutes, uncovered, to intensify the flavor.

7. Meanwhile, when the chicken is cool enough to handle, discard the skin and the bones. Cut the chicken meat into large pieces and refrigerate with the carrots. You can use the chicken in the soup, or save it for salads or sandwiches.

8. When the stock has finished cooking and is cool enough to handle, pour it through the strainer into the other bowl and refrigerate it for 5 or 6 hours, or overnight, to solidify the fat. With the large spoon scrape the fat off the top of the soup and discard it. Reheat the soup in the large pot.

The stock may also be frozen for later use.

Chicken-in-the-Pot: Add the chicken pieces, carrots, and 1 cup of cooked egg noodles to the soup, and heat.

Breads, Biscuits, Muffins, and More

Cheddar Cheese Crisps

You can make the dough for these tangy cheese appetizers and keep it in the freezer, ready to slice and bake in minutes.

Makes about 20 to 30 1½-inch rounds

Ingredients

For preparing the baking sheets:
2 teaspoons butter
For the dough:
4 ounces sharp Cheddar
    cheese
4 tablespoons (½ stick)
    butter, very soft
1 teaspoon dry mustard
½ teaspoon salt
½ cup flour

Equipment

Measuring cups
Measuring spoons
Grater
Waxed paper
Large mixing bowl
Wooden spoon
Pastry board
Plastic wrap or foil
2 cookie sheets
Serrated knife
Oven mitts
Spatula
Cake rack

1. Stand the grater on a sheet of waxed paper and grate the cheese finely, using the side with the smallest holes.

2. In the large mixing bowl beat the softened butter with the wooden spoon until creamy. Add the grated cheese, mustard, and salt and mix together until well blended.

3. With the wooden spoon beat in the flour, 2 tablespoons at a time, mixing well after each addition. Gather the dough into a ball.

4. Lightly flour the pastry board. Shape the cheese ball into a log about 1½ inches in diameter. Wrap the log in plastic wrap or foil and chill in the refrigerator until firm, at least an hour or two. (If you aren't going to bake the cheese crisps now, you can keep the unbaked log, tightly wrapped, in the refrigerator for several weeks or in the freezer.)

5. Preheat the oven to 375°F. and butter the cookie sheets.

6. With the serrated knife, slice the chilled or frozen cheese log into thin rounds no more than ¼ inch thick, and place them an inch apart on the prepared cookie sheets. Bake for 7 to 10 minutes, or just until the edges start to turn golden. Keep an eye on them as they scorch easily.

7. Wearing the oven mitts, take the baked crisps out of the oven. Remove them from the baking sheets with the spatula, and let them cool on the cake rack. They will keep fresh for a week in a tightly covered canister.

Baking Powder Biscuits

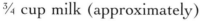

These are crisp on the outside, flaky and delectable. Serve them hot with butter. For breakfast, try putting ½ teaspoon of orange marmalade on each biscuit before baking. If you have any left over, heat them in a microwave for 30 seconds, or split and top-brown them for a few minutes under the broiler.

Makes 12 to 15 2-inch biscuits

Ingredients
2 cups flour
4 teaspoons baking powder
1 teaspoon salt
4 tablespoons (½ stick)
    butter
¾ cup milk (approximately)

Equipment
Measuring cups
Measuring spoons
Sifter
Mixing bowl
Pastry blender or 2 dull
    knives
Fork
Pastry board
Rolling pin
2-inch cookie cutter or glass
    2 inches in diameter
Cookie sheets, ungreased
Oven mitts

1. Preheat the oven to 450°F.

2. Sift the flour, baking powder, and salt into the mixing bowl.

Add the butter and cut it into the flour with the pastry blender or the knives until the granules are about the size of peas.

3. Add the milk a little at a time, mixing with the fork until the dough is soft but not sticky and forms a ball. You may not need all the milk.

4. Sprinkle the pastry board lightly with flour and turn the ball of dough out in the center of it. Lightly flour the rolling pin and roll the dough out in short quick strokes in every direction, taking care not to press down heavily, until it's about ½ inch thick all over.

5. With the 2-inch cookie cutter or the glass cut out rounds from the dough and place them on the cookie sheets. Press the scraps of leftover dough together, roll out again, and cut out more biscuits as before.

6. Bake about 12 to 15 minutes, or until the tops are golden.

7. Wearing the oven mitts, remove the biscuits from the oven. Serve immediately.

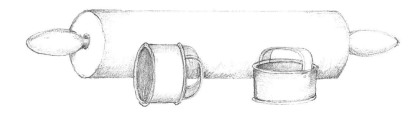

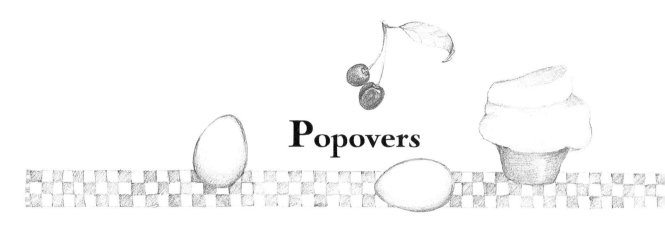

Popovers

Popovers are crisp on the outside, moist and tender inside, and must be served right out of the oven.

Makes 8 large popovers

Ingredients	Equipment
For preparing the pans:	Muffin tin or 8 ovenproof
1 tablespoon butter	glass cups
For the batter:	Measuring cups
2 eggs	Measuring spoons
1 cup milk	Small saucepan to melt
1 tablespoon butter, melted,	butter
at room temperature	Electric mixer and bowl
1 cup flour	Large spoon
¼ teaspoon salt	Oven mitts

1. Preheat the oven to 450°F. Butter 8 cups of the muffin tin or the 8 glass cups.

2. With the electric mixer beat the eggs in the mixing bowl until frothy. With the mixer on low speed stir in the milk, melted butter, flour, and salt and beat just until blended and the mixture looks like heavy cream. Don't overbeat.

3. Using the large spoon, fill the muffin cups or glass cups ⅓ full. Bake 20 minutes, reduce the oven heat to 350°F., and bake 15 to

60

20 minutes longer, or until the popovers are brown and crisp and the tops have puffed way up.

4. Wearing the oven mitts, remove the popovers from the oven. Turn the muffin tin or glass cups on their sides and let the popovers fall out. If any are stuck, loosen them around the sides with a knife.

5. Serve immediately, with butter and jam.

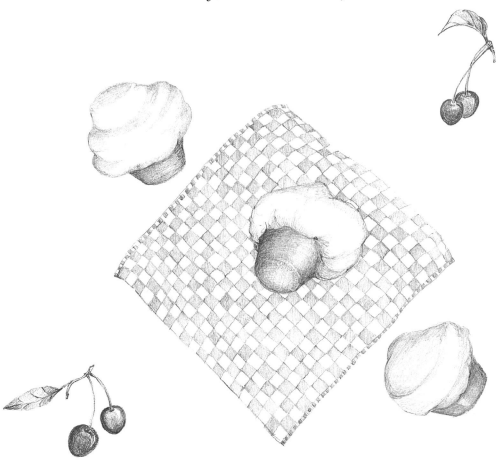

Corn Bread

This is a good old-fashioned recipe for corn bread, a staple of the early settlers. Serve it warm.

Makes 16 2-inch squares

Ingredients
For preparing the baking pan:
1 to 2 teaspoons butter
For the batter:
1 cup flour
⅓ cup sugar
1 tablespoon baking powder
¾ teaspoon salt
¾ cup yellow cornmeal
1 egg
1 cup milk
2 tablespoons butter, melted

Equipment
8-inch-square baking pan
Measuring cups
Measuring spoons
Small saucepan to melt
   butter
Sifter
Large mixing bowl
Wooden spoon
Small bowl
Rotary hand beater
Rubber spatula
Cake tester
Oven mitts

1. Preheat the oven to 425°F. Butter the baking pan.

2. Sift the flour, sugar, baking powder, and salt together into the large mixing bowl. Stir in the cornmeal with the wooden spoon.

3. In the small bowl beat the egg well with the rotary hand beater, then stir in the milk and the melted butter.

4. Pour the liquid ingredients over the cornmeal mixture and mix the batter well with the wooden spoon. Pour it into the prepared pan, using the rubber spatula to scrape the sides of the mixing bowl.

5. Bake for about 20 minutes, or until the cake tester inserted in the center comes out clean. Wearing the oven mitts, remove the bread from the oven.

6. Let the bread cool for about 10 minutes, then cut it into 2-inch squares and serve. You can wrap leftover corn bread in foil and reheat it in a warm oven.

Banana Bread

Makes one 9 × 5-inch loaf

Ingredients

For preparing the baking pan:
1 to 2 teaspoons butter
For the batter:
8 tablespoons (1 stick)
    butter, softened
1 cup sugar
2 eggs
2 cups flour
1 teaspoon baking soda
½ teaspoon salt
¼ cup milk
1 cup mashed ripe bananas
    (about 2 big or 3 small)
½ cup chopped walnuts

Equipment

9 × 5-inch loaf pan
Measuring cups
Measuring spoons
Electric mixer
Sifter
Large mixing bowls
Mixing spoon
Rubber spatula
Oven mitts
Cake tester
Cake rack

1. Preheat the oven to 350°F. and butter the loaf pan.

2. With the electric mixer, or by hand, cream the butter in one mixing bowl until soft and light. Beat in the sugar, a little at a time, until the mixture is fluffy. Beat in the eggs.

3. Sift together the flour, baking soda, and salt into another mixing bowl. With the mixer on low speed, add half the flour mixture to the batter, then the milk, then the remaining flour.

4. With the mixing spoon stir in the mashed bananas and the chopped walnuts.

5. Spoon the batter into the prepared pan, using the rubber spatula to scrape the sides of the bowl. Bake for 60 minutes, or until the cake tester inserted in the middle comes out clean. With oven mitts on, remove the bread from the oven.

6. Let the bread cool in the pan for 10 minutes. Put the mitts back on and tip the loaf pan on its side over the cake rack to let the banana bread fall out on the rack. Cool right side up on the cake rack.

Raisin Muffins

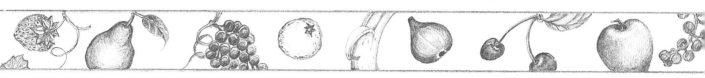

This is a basic muffin recipe for a breakfast treat that is really easy and quick to make. If you like dates, you can substitute them for the raisins.

Makes 12 muffins

Ingredients
2 cups flour
1 tablespoon baking powder
1 teaspoon salt
¼ cup sugar
1 egg
1 cup milk
4 tablespoons (½ stick) butter, melted and cooled
½ cup raisins (or pitted dates, cut into small pieces with a wet scissors)

Equipment
Muffin tin
Paper baking cups
Measuring cups
Measuring spoons
Small saucepan to melt butter
Sifter
Large mixing bowl
Small mixing bowl
Whisk
Mixing spoon
Oven mitts

1. Preheat oven to 400°F. Line each cup of the muffin tin with a paper baking cup.

2. Sift the flour, baking powder, salt, and sugar together into the large mixing bowl.

3. In the small mixing bowl beat the egg with a whisk until frothy, then whisk in the milk and melted butter.

4. Pour the egg mixture over the flour and stir with the large spoon just enough to dampen the flour. Don't beat; the batter isn't supposed to be smooth.

5. Stir in the raisins and spoon the batter into the paper baking cups in the muffin tin, filling each one about ⅔ full. Bake about 18 to 20 minutes, or until the tops are dry and the muffins shrink slightly from the cups.

6. With oven mitts on, remove the muffin tin from the oven and turn out the muffins.

Blueberry Muffins

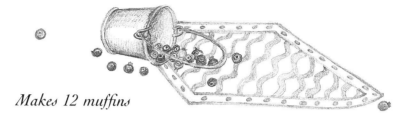

Makes 12 muffins

Ingredients

1 cup blueberries
1¾ cups plus 2 tablespoons
    flour
1 tablespoon baking powder
1 teaspoon salt
½ cup sugar
1 egg
1 cup milk
4 tablespoons (½ stick)
    butter, melted and
    cooled

Equipment

Muffin tin
Paper baking cups
Measuring cups
Measuring spoons
Small saucepan to melt
    butter
Small bowl
Colander
Sifter
Large mixing bowl
Small mixing bowl
Whisk
Mixing spoon
Oven mitts

1. Preheat oven to 400°F. Line each cup of the muffin tin with a paper baking cup.

2. Wash and drain the blueberries in the colander, pick out any stems or leaves, and set the berries aside in the small bowl.

68

3. Sift 1¾ cups of the flour, the baking powder, salt, and sugar together into the large mixing bowl.

4. In the small mixing bowl beat the egg with a whisk until frothy, then whisk in the milk and melted butter.

5. Pour the egg mixture over the flour and stir with the mixing spoon only enough to dampen the flour. Don't beat; the batter isn't supposed to be smooth.

6. Sprinkle the remaining 2 tablespoons of flour over the blue-berries, and fold them into the batter. Spoon the batter into the paper baking cups in the muffin tin, filling each one about ⅔ full. Bake about 18 to 20 minutes, or until the tops are dry and the muffins shrink slightly from the sides of the cups.

7. Wearing the oven mitts, remove the muffin tin from the oven and turn out the muffins.

Applesauce Muffins

Makes 16 muffins

Ingredients

8 tablespoons (1 stick)
    butter
1 cup brown sugar
1 egg
2 cups flour
1 teaspoon baking powder
1 teaspoon baking soda
½ teaspoon salt
1 teaspoon cinnamon
½ teaspoon powdered ginger
    or cloves
1 cup applesauce
½ cup raisins
½ cup chopped nuts

Equipment

2 muffin tins
Paper baking cups
Measuring cups
Measuring spoons
Electric mixer
Mixing bowl
Sifter
Small bowl
Large spoon
Oven mitts
Cake tester

1. Preheat oven to 350°F. Line 16 cups of the muffin tins with paper baking cups.

2. With the electric mixer cream the butter in the mixing bowl until soft and light. Beat in the sugar, a little at a time, until the mixture is fluffy. Beat in the egg.

70

3. Sift together the flour, baking powder, baking soda, salt, cinnamon, and ginger or cloves into the small bowl, and mix them into the batter on low speed.

4. With the large spoon stir in the applesauce, raisins, and chopped nuts.

5. Spoon the batter into the prepared muffin tins, filling each ⅔ full. Bake about 20 minutes, or until the muffins are golden and the cake tester comes out clean.

6. Wearing the oven mitts, remove the muffin tin from the oven and turn out remove the muffins.

Peanut Butter Bread

Makes one 9 × 5-inch loaf

Ingredients

For preparing the baking pan:
1 to 2 teaspoons butter
For the batter:
2 cups flour
⅓ cup sugar
2 teaspoons baking powder
1 teaspoon salt
1 egg
1 cup milk
¾ cup chunky peanut butter

Equipment

9 × 5-inch loaf pan
Measuring cups
Measuring spoons
Sifter
Large mixing bowl
Small mixing bowl
Rotary hand beater
Mixing spoon
Mixing fork
Oven mitts
Cake rack

1. Preheat the oven to 350°F. and butter the loaf pan.

2. Sift the flour, sugar, baking powder, and salt together into the large mixing bowl.

3. In the small mixing bowl beat the egg with the rotary hand beater until frothy and stir in the milk.

4. Stir the milk-egg mixture and the peanut butter into the flour mixture with the fork, working them in until well blended.

1. Butter the loaf pan.

2. Pour the warm water into the small mixing bowl, sprinkle it with the dry yeast, and stir until mixed.

3. In a large mixing bowl, lightly beat the egg with the rotary hand beater. Add the cottage cheese, sugar, onion flakes, and melted butter and combine well. Mix in the dill, salt, baking soda, and yeast mixture.

4. Add about 2¼ cups of the flour, and stir with the wooden spoon. Then stir in more flour, a tablespoon at a time, just until the dough becomes too stiff to mix and comes away from the sides of the bowl.

5. Sprinkle the pastry board with a little flour, place the ball of dough in the center of it, and sprinkle a little flour on the top of the dough. Place the heels of your hands at the near side of the dough, and push the dough away from you. Bring the far edge of the dough back toward you and fold it over the near edge. Turn the dough a quarter of a circle so the fold is now at one side, then push the dough away from you again. Repeat the process of pushing, folding, and turning the dough — this is called kneading — for about 10 minutes. If the dough gets too sticky to work, sprinkle a little flour over it.

6. With a little vegetable oil, lightly grease the bottom and sides of another clean, large mixing bowl. Put the dough in the bowl and turn the dough to oil it all over. Cover the bowl with the clean dry dish towel, set it in a warm place, and let the dough rise until is has doubled its size, about 1 hour.

7. Punch the dough down in the middle, and turn it out on the lightly floured pastry board. Knead the dough lightly for a minute or two, then pat it into a loaf shape.

8. Put the dough into the prepared loaf pan. Sprinkle the top evenly with the dill seeds.

9. Preheat the oven to 375°F., and let the dough rest in the pan until the oven is ready.

10. Bake for about 45 minutes, or until the top of the bread is golden brown and feels firm.

11. Remove the pan carefully, wearing the oven mitts, and turn it on its side so the bread falls out. Cool the loaf on the cake rack right side up.

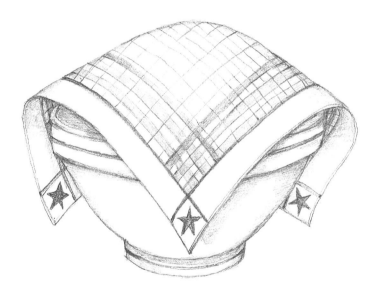

Rye Bread

Makes 2 loaves

Ingredients

For preparing the cookie sheet:
1 to 2 teaspoons butter
For the dough:
2 tablespoons molasses
2 tablespoons butter,
     softened
2 teaspoons salt
1 cup milk
1 cup warm water
1 package dry yeast
3½ to 4 cups white flour
2 tablespoons caraway seeds
2 cups rye flour
1 to 2 tablespoons vegetable
     oil

Equipment

Cookie sheet
Measuring cups
Measuring spoons
2 large mixing bowls
Small saucepan
Wooden spoon
Small mixing bowl
Mixing spoon
Pastry board
Clean dry dish towel
Knife
Oven mitts
Cake rack

1. Butter the cookie sheet.

2. Put the molasses, softened butter, and salt in a large mixing bowl.

3. In the saucepan bring the milk almost to a boil, then pour it

over the molasses and butter and stir with the wooden spoon until the mixture is blended. Let it cool.

4. In the small mixing bowl put 1 cup of warm water and sprinkle the yeast over it. Stir until the yeast is dissolved and add it to the milk mixture.

5. Add in 3½ cups of the white flour and the caraway seeds and stir until smooth. Gradually add in the rye flour, stirring until the dough is stiff. Form the dough into a ball.

6. Sprinkle the pastry board with a little of the remaining white flour, place the ball of dough in the center of it, and sprinkle a little more flour over the dough. Place the heels of your hands at the near side of the dough, and push the dough away from you. Bring the far edge of the dough back toward you and fold it over the near edge. Turn the dough a quarter of a circle so the fold is now at one side, then push the dough away from you again. Repeat the process of pushing, folding, and turning the dough — this is called kneading — for about 10 minutes, or until the dough is smooth and shiny. If the dough gets too sticky to work, sprinkle a little more white flour over it.

7. With a little vegetable oil, lightly grease the bottom and sides of another clean, large mixing bowl. Put the dough in the bowl and turn the dough to oil it all over. Cover the bowl with the clean dry dish towel, set it in a warm place, and let the dough rise until it has doubled its size, about 1 to 2 hours.

8. Punch the dough down in the middle and turn it out on the lightly floured pastry board. Divide it in two with the knife and shape each half into an oblong loaf.

9. Put the loaves on each end of the prepared baking sheet, cover

them with the dish towel, and let them rise again until they are twice their size, about an hour.

10. Preheat the oven to 375°F.

11. Bake the bread for about 40 or 45 minutes, until it looks done, then remove it carefully, wearing the oven mitts. Turn one of the loaves on its side, and thump it on the bottom with your knuckles. If you don't hear a hollow sound, put the loaves back in the oven to bake another 5 minutes or so, then test them again. When the bread is done, cool it on a cake rack right side up.

Meat and Fish

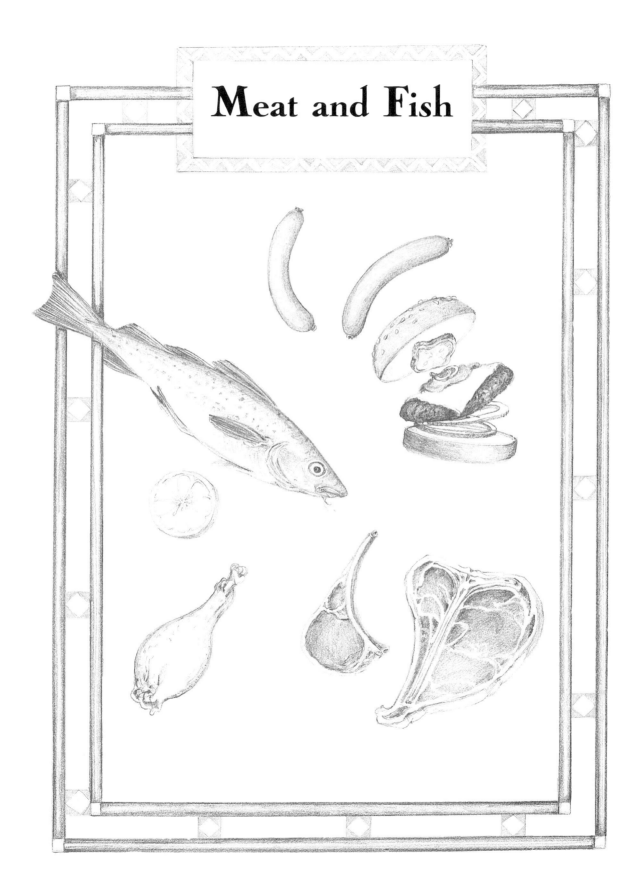

Hot Dogs

Hot dogs, more formally called frankfurters, can be all beef, or a combination of beef and other meats, and sometimes have nonmeat fillers as well. Figure 2 per person, and serve on lightly toasted frankfurter rolls with your favorite accompaniments, such as mustard, sauerkraut, sweet relish.

Serves 4

Ingredients
8 hot dogs
For panfrying:
1 tablespoon butter

Equipment
To boil:
4-quart saucepan
Tongs
To panfry:
12-inch skillet
Small knife
Tongs
To broil:
Broiler pan with a rack
Oven mitts
Tongs

1. *To boil:* Bring 2 quarts of water to a boil in the saucepan, lower the heat, add the hot dogs, and simmer for 4 to 5 minutes. Don't worry if the hot dog casings split. Remove with tongs and serve in hot dog rolls.

82

2. *To panfry:* Melt the butter over moderate heat in the skillet. With the small knife make 4 or 5 shallow diagonal cuts along the top of the hot dogs, and, turning them with tongs, panfry about 3 minutes on each side, or until they are brown.

3. *To broil:* Preheat the broiler. Place the hot dogs on the rack in the broiler pan. Put the pan about 2 inches from the source of heat and broil about 2 minutes on each side, or until well browned. Wear oven mitts to pull the broiler pan out and use tongs to turn the hot dogs over.

Variation

Split each hot dog lengthwise, almost but not quite through, tuck in thin strips of American cheese, wind a strip of bacon around each hot dog, and broil until the bacon is crisp.

Hamburgers

The best hamburgers are panfried, like these, or charcoal-grilled; broil them only if they are at least 1½ to 2 inches thick. Good-quality beef makes sweet, juicy burgers, delicious alone, or served on lightly toasted hamburger buns, English muffins, or rolls, with catsup, mustard, slices of sweet Bermuda onions, and sliced tomatoes on the side.

Serves 4

Ingredients
1⅓ pounds ground beef, half chuck and half sirloin
1 teaspoon salt
Freshly ground pepper
1 tablespoon vegetable oil
2 tablespoons butter

Equipment
Mixing bowl
Measuring spoons
12-inch cast-iron skillet
Slotted spatula
Serving platter
Wooden spoon

1. Put the ground beef in the mixing bowl and add the salt and a few grindings of pepper. Lightly combine them with your hands. Divide the meat into quarters and lightly shape each quarter into a patty about ½ inch thick. Handle gently so the meat will not be pressed solid.

2. Heat the oil and 1 tablespoon of the butter over high heat in the skillet until the fats are hot but not smoking, then add the hamburger patties. Turn the heat down a little and panfry the patties 6 to 7 minutes on each side until they are well done,

turning them with the slotted spatula. Watch them carefully; overcooking dries out chopped meat and pressing them down squeezes the juice out.

3. Meanwhile, warm the serving platter in a slow oven. When the hamburgers are cooked, transfer them to the warm platter with the spatula.

4. Add the remaining 1 tablespoon of butter to the juices in the frying pan, scrape the bottom of the pan with the wooden spoon, and combine the pan drippings with the butter. Drizzle over the hamburgers.

Variations

Cheeseburgers: After the hamburgers are done, cover each patty with a round of cheddar cheese and partially cover the frying pan with a lid for a minute or two, until the cheese melts. For a more piquant flavor, spread a teaspoon of Dijon mustard or chili sauce over each patty before adding the cheese.

Hamburger Toast: Preheat broiler. Put 4 slices of bread on a cookie sheet and toast in the broiler on one side. Remove from the broiler and cover the untoasted sides with the ground beef. Broil for 5 minutes, dot the tops with about 1 tablespoon of cut-up butter, and serve.

Meat Loaf

This is a basic recipe for meat loaf, which you can modify in many ways, as you'll see under **Variations,** below. Whichever ingredients you choose, use fresh, raw meat because leftover cooked meat makes a dry meat loaf. Thinly sliced cold meat loaf makes wonderful sandwiches.

Serves 8

Ingredients
1 teaspoon butter to butter
    loaf pan
1 egg
2 pounds ground beef
½ cup freshly made Bread
    Crumbs (page 2)
½ cup milk
1 onion, peeled and finely
    chopped
1 teaspoon salt
Freshly ground pepper
¼ teaspoon ground nutmeg
2 slices bacon
Tomato Sauce (page 150),
    optional

Equipment
9 × 5-inch loaf pan or foil
    loaf pan
Measuring cups
Measuring spoons
Large mixing bowl
Fork
Oven mitts

1. Preheat the oven to 350°F. and butter the loaf pan, or use a foil loaf pan, unbuttered.

2. In the large mixing bowl beat the egg slightly with the fork, then add all the ingredients except the bacon and combine them well with a kitchen fork or your hands. Pat the mixture into the prepared loaf pan and smooth the top with your hands. Lay the bacon strips lengthwise over the meat and bake for 45 to 60 minutes, or until the loaf is firm.

3. Carefully remove the loaf from the oven, wearing oven mitts, and turn out onto a heated platter. Serve with Tomato Sauce, if desired.

Variations

Mixed Meat Loaf: Instead of all beef, use ⅓ ground beef, ⅓ ground veal, ⅓ ground pork, and substitute beef stock for the milk.

Spicy Meat Loaf: Add 2 tablespoons Worcestershire sauce or 2 tablespoons horseradish and 1 teaspoon garlic salt and substitute tomato juice for the milk.

Vegetable Veal Loaf: Use all veal and add one 10-ounce package of frozen spinach, defrosted and squeezed dry, ¼ cup finely chopped parsley, ¼ cup snipped dill, and 1 teaspoon dried thyme.

Chili

This is an easy-to-make, do-ahead dish that everyone likes. You can double the receipe for a crowd of friends. Serve it with Steamed Rice (page 165) and corn chips.

Serves 6

Ingredients

2 tablespoons vegetable oil
3 cloves garlic, peeled
2 onions, peeled and finely
    chopped
1½ pounds lean ground beef
3 tablespoons chili powder
1 teaspoon celery salt
1 tablespoon ground cumin
1 tablespoon dried oregano
1 35-ounce can Italian-style
    tomatoes
2 16-ounce cans red kidney
    beans

Equipment

Measuring spoons
Heavy 3- or 5-quart cast-
    iron casserole
Garlic press
Wooden spoon
Kitchen spoon or bulb baster
Colander

1. In the casserole heat the oil over medium heat. Press the garlic cloves through a garlic press into the hot oil, add the chopped onions, and sauté about 5 to 6 minutes, or until they are translucent and soft, stirring occasionally with the wooden spoon.

2. Add the ground beef, break it up with the spoon, and spread it around the pan. Sauté the meat, stirring it frequently, until it is well done and no pink color remains. Push the meat mixture to one side; with a kitchen spoon or bulb baster remove and discard as much fat and oil as you can.

3. Stir in the chili powder, celery salt, cumin, and oregano and cook for 2 to 3 minutes.

4. Add the tomatoes, turn the heat to low, and simmer, un-covered, for 2 hours, or until the mixture is thick, stirring occasionally.

5. Drain the kidney beans through the colander into the sink and stir them into the chili. Cook for 10 more minutes, or until the kidney beans are heated.

6. Serve the chili right out of the casserole, or transfer it to a heated serving bowl.

Broiled Steak

The best cuts for broiling are sirloin, club, porterhouse, T-bone, and rib steaks that are 1 to 2 inches thick. Thinner steaks should be panfried (see page 92). Figure on up to ½ pound of meat per person and twice as much per person of bone-in steak.

Ingredients
1 steak
Salt
Freshly ground pepper

Equipment
Cutting board for meat
Knife
Roasting pan with flat rack
Foil
Tongs or a long-handled fork
Oven mitts
Carving board
Carving knife
Two-pronged fork

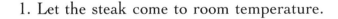

1. Let the steak come to room temperature.

2. Before heating the broiler, set the oven shelf so that when the steak is on the roasting pan rack the top surface of the steak is 2 inches from the source of heat for a 1-inch-thick steak, 3 inches for a 1½-inch steak, and 4 inches for a 2-inch steak. Turn the broiler to its highest setting and preheat it for 15 minutes.

3. Place the steak on the cutting board and trim off most of the fat, leaving only a narrow edge all around. Notch the remaining

fat every inch or so to prevent the edges of the steak from curling up. Lay the steak on the cold roasting pan rack. To simplify cleanup, line the bottom of the pan with foil.

4. Slide the pan with rack into the broiler. Broil a 1-inch-thick steak 4 to 5 minutes on each side for rare, 6 to 7 minutes for medium, and 8 to 9 minutes for well done. Broil a 1½-inch steak 5 to 6 minutes per side for rare, 7 to 8 minutes for medium, and 9 to 10 minutes for well done. Broil a 2-inch-thick steak 6 to 7 minutes on each side for rare, 8 to 9 minutes for medium, and 10 to 11 minutes per side for well done. Turn the steak over with tongs or the long-handled fork, wearing oven mitts to pull out the broiler pan.

5. Transfer the steak to the carving board and lightly salt and pepper it. Anchoring the steak with a two-pronged fork, cut around the bone with the tip of the carving knife, and remove it. Then cut the steak against the grain into half-inch slices. Transfer to a heated platter or individual plates and serve.

THICKNESS	RARE	MEDIUM	WELL DONE
1 inch	4 to 5 minutes each side	6 to 7 minutes each side	8 to 9 minutes each side
1½ inches	5 to 6 minutes each side	7 to 8 minutes each side	9 to 10 minutes each side
2 inches	6 to 7 minutes each side	8 to 9 minutes each side	10 to 11 minutes each side

Panfried Steak

When a steak is less than 1 inch thick, panfrying is the cooking method of choice; broiling would overcook it. This method works for any cut of steak, including thin sirloins and porterhouses, and is particularly useful for minute steaks and fillets. Figure on ½ pound of meat per person.

Ingredients
1 or more steaks
2 tablespoons vegetable oil
1 tablespoon butter
Salt
Freshly ground pepper

Equipment
Cutting board for meat
Knife
Paper towels
Heavy 12-inch cast-iron
    skillet
Tongs
Carving board

1. Let the steak come to room temperature. Place on the cutting board and trim off most of the fat, leaving only a narrow edge all around. Notch the remaining fat every inch or so to prevent the edges of the steak from curling up. Pat the steak dry with paper towels.

2. In the heavy skillet heat the oil and butter over high heat until they are very hot but not smoking, and the butter is beginning to get faintly brown. Lower the heat to medium and panfry the steak on one side for 1 minute. Turn it over with the tongs and panfry the other side for 1 minute. Repeat this process two more

times, cooking the steak for a total of 6 minutes for rare steak. Cook another minute or two on each side for medium steak.

3. Transfer the steak to the carving board for slicing, or a heated serving platter, and lightly salt and pepper it.

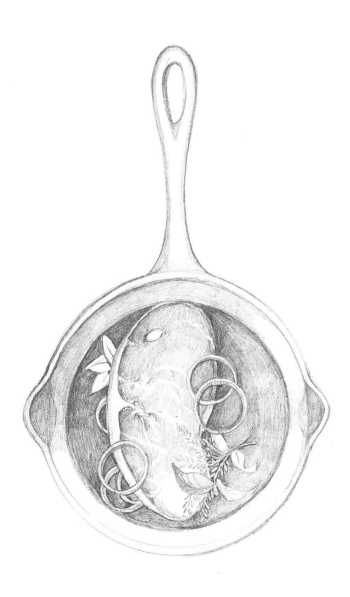

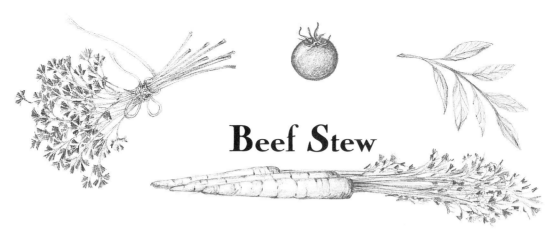

Beef Stew

This is another crowd pleaser that tastes even better the second day. The moist-heat method of cooking makes tougher cuts of meat tender and succulent.

Serves 6

Ingredients	**Equipment**
2 pounds beef chuck	Cutting board for meat
4 tablespoons vegetable oil	Knife
1 medium onion, peeled and coarsely chopped	Paper towels
¼ cup flour	Heavy 5-quart cast-iron casserole with cover
½ teaspoon salt	Measuring cups
2 tablespoons butter	Measuring spoons
1 35-ounce can Italian-style tomatoes	Wooden spoon
¼ cup finely chopped parsley	Large slotted spoon
2 bay leaves	Large mixing bowl
1 bunch carrots	Large plastic bag
12 small white onions	Tongs
6 new potatoes	Waxed paper
Salt	Vegetable peeler
Freshly ground pepper	Small mixing bowl

1. Lay the meat on the cutting board and cut it into 1½-inch cubes. Dry the pieces well with paper towels.

2. In the casserole heat 2 tablespoons of the oil, add the chopped onions, and sauté over moderate heat about 5 to 6 minutes, or until the onions are translucent and soft, stirring occasionally with the wooden spoon. With the large slotted spoon, transfer the onions to the large mixing bowl and set aside.

3. Pour the flour and salt into the large plastic bag, hold the opening tightly closed with your hand, and shake to combine them. Drop a few cubes of meat into the plastic bag, hold the opening tightly closed, and shake the bag to flour the meat on all sides. Remove the meat cubes one at a time with tongs and shake them over the bag to remove all excess flour. Set the floured meat aside on a piece of waxed paper. Repeat the process until all the cubes of meat have been lightly floured. If you run out of flour, combine another ¼ cup of flour and ½ teaspoon of salt in the plastic bag. Don't flour the meat until you are ready to brown it, because the flour coating gets gummy if it sits around.

4. Heat the remaining 2 tablespoons of oil and the butter in the casserole over high heat and brown the meat, a few pieces at a time, turning them with tongs to brown them on all sides. As each piece is browned, transfer it with tongs to the mixing bowl with the onions. When all the pieces are browned, return the meat and onions to the casserole.

5. Add the tomatoes, parsley, and bay leaves to the casserole, turn the heat down, cover, and simmer about 1½ to 2 hours, or until the meat is tender when pierced with the tip of a knife.

6. Meanwhile, scrape the carrots with the vegetable peeler and cut them crosswise into 1-inch lengths. Put them aside in the small mixing bowl. Trim the white onions, peel the new potatoes with the vegetable peeler, and add both to the carrots.

7. When the meat is tender, add the carrots, white onions, and

new potatoes and simmer for about 15 to 20 minutes, or until you can pierce them easily with the point of a knife.

8. Taste the stew for seasoning and add salt and pepper, if necessary. Serve from the casserole.

Broiled Lamb Chops

Loin chops, rib chops, and shoulder chops can all be broiled if they are at least an inch thick, and they are particularly good when they are cut as double-thick chops. Thinner chops should be panfried (see page 99). Figure on 2 single chops or 1 double chop per person.

Ingredients
Lamb chops
Salt
Freshly ground pepper

Equipment
Cutting board for meat
Knife
Roasting pan with flat rack
Foil
Tongs
Oven mitts

1. Let the chops come to room temperature.

2. Before heating the broiler, set the oven shelf so that when the chops are on the roasting pan rack the top surface of the chops is 2 inches from the source of heat for single (1-inch-thick) chops, and 4 inches for double (2-inch-thick) chops. Turn the broiler to its highest setting and preheat it for 15 minutes.

3. Place the chops on the cutting board and trim off most of the fat, leaving only a narrow edge all around. Notch the remaining fat every inch or so to prevent the edges of the chops from curling up. Lay the chops on the cold roasting pan rack. To simplify cleanup, line the bottom of the pan with foil.

4. Slide the pan with rack into the broiler. Broil single chops 5 to 6 minutes on each side for medium, 7 to 8 minutes for well done. Broil double 2-inch thick chops 7 to 8 minutes for medium, 9 to 10 minutes for well done. Turn the chops over with tongs, wearing oven mitts to pull out the broiler pan.

5. Transfer the chops to a heated platter and serve.

THICKNESS	MEDIUM	WELL DONE
single chop (1 inch thick)	5 to 6 minutes each side	7 to 8 minutes each side
double chop (2 inches thick)	7 to 8 minutes each side	9 to 10 minutes each side

Panfried Lamb Chops

When a chop is less than 1 inch thick, panfrying is the cooking method of choice; broiling would overcook it. Figure on 2 single chops per person.

Ingredients
Thin lamb chops
2 tablespoons vegetable oil
1 tablespoon butter
Salt
Freshly ground pepper

Equipment
Cutting board for meat
Knife
Paper towels
Heavy 12-inch cast-iron
   skillet
Tongs
Serving platter

1. Let the chops come to room temperature. Place on the cutting board and trim off most of the fat, leaving only a narrow edge all around. Notch the remaining fat every inch or so to prevent the edges of the chops from curling up. Pat them dry with paper towels.

2. In the heavy skillet heat the oil and butter over high heat until very hot but not smoking, and the butter is beginning to get faintly brown. Lower the heat to medium and panfry the chops on one side for 1 minute. Turn them over with tongs and panfry them on the other side for 1 minute. Repeat this process, cooking the chops a minute or two more on one side and then the other, for a total of 6 minutes.

3. Transfer the chops to the heated serving platter and lightly salt and pepper them.

4. If you have more chops than fit into the frying pan at one time, you can panfry two batches at the same time, or keep the first batch warm on the heated serving platter in a slow oven while you panfry the rest of them.

Baked Ham

A glazed baked ham has just about everything going for it — it couldn't be easier to cook, it serves a crowd of friends at a party or a big family for a holiday meal, it's delicious freshly baked and superb as a leftover in sandwiches, omelets, quiches, salads, biscuits. You can get half a ham, but a whole ham, with bone in, seems to cook up better. Boned hams and canned hams are easy to carve but lack rich flavor. Figure around ¾ to 1 pound of ham per person.

Ingredients
1 ham, bone in, 10 to 14
    pounds
1¼ cups orange juice
1 cup brown sugar
1 tablespoon dry mustard
1 cup fresh bread crumbs

Equipment
Large roasting pan
Collapsible V-shaped rack
Measuring cups
Measuring spoons
Bulb baster or large spoon
Small mixing bowl
Oven mitts
Knife
Rubber spatula
Instant meat thermometer

1. Preheat oven to 325°F.

2. Set the V-shaped rack in the large roasting pan and place the ham in it, fat side up. Slide it into the oven. Bake the ham for 15 minutes a pound, or about 2½ to 3 hours. Baste it every half hour, using the bulb baster or large spoon, with 1 cup of the orange juice.

3. While the ham is baking, prepare the glaze. In the small mixing bowl combine the brown sugar, dry mustard, and bread crumbs. Moisten the mixture with the remaining ¼ cup orange juice, adding it a tablespoonful at a time.

4. When the ham has baked for about 3 hours, move the roasting pan to a heatproof countertop or the top of the stove, wearing the oven mitts. Cut shallow diagonal slashes across the fat side of the ham, forming a diamond pattern. With the rubber spatula spread the glaze over the slashed side of the ham, spooning up and reapplying any glaze that slides off into the pan.

5. With oven mitts on, put the ham back into the oven and, without basting, bake for 30 to 45 minutes, or until the meat thermometer registers 160°F.

6. Wearing oven mitts, put the roasting pan on a heatproof counter and transfer the ham to a heated serving platter. Let it sit 15 or 20 minutes before carving it.

Roast Chicken

Any plump young chicken is fine for roasting, whether it's called a roaster, broiler, or fryer. Figure about 1 pound per person.

Ingredients

1 3- to 5-pound chicken
½ lemon, cut into 2 quarters
Salt
4 tablespoons butter (½ stick), softened
Freshly ground pepper
½ to 1 cup chicken stock

Equipment

Measuring spoons
Measuring cups
Paper towels
Cutting board for meat
Roasting pan
Collapsible V-shaped rack
Small saucepan
Bulb baster
Instant meat thermometer
Oven mitts
Wooden spoon

1. Preheat the oven to 400°F.

2. As soon as you unwrap the chicken, remove the neck and the bag of giblets from the body cavities and freeze for another use or discard.

3. Wash the chicken thoroughly under cold water, inside and out, and pat dry with paper towels. Place on the cutting board. Rub one of the lemon quarters inside the body cavity and rub the other over the skin of the chicken. Set the lemon aside. Rub ½ teaspoon of salt into the body cavity. Rub 2 tablespoons of the

softened butter over the skin and sprinkle with ½ teaspoon salt and a few grindings of pepper.

4. Place the chicken breast side up on the V-shaped rack in the roasting pan and put it in the preheated oven.

5. Wash your hands, the cutting board, and any utensils that touched the raw chicken in hot soapy water and dry well.

6. In the small saucepan melt the remaining 2 tablespoons of butter over low heat and squeeze into it whatever juice remains in the lemon quarters.

7. After the chicken has cooked for 15 minutes, pour the lemon butter over it and continue to cook, basting with a bulb baster every 15 minutes. When the chicken has cooked for 1 hour, briefly poke the thermometer into the thigh without touching the bone; it will register 175°F. if the chicken is done. If not, continue cooking and test every 5 minutes.

8. Wearing oven mitts, take the roasting pan out of the oven, transfer the chicken to a heated serving platter, and let it rest.

9. Remove the rack and place the roasting pan on top of the stove over high heat. Pour ½ cup of the chicken stock into the pan and scrape the crusty drippings from the bottom of the pan with a wooden spoon, combining them with the stock to deglaze the pan and turn the delicious drippings into a little pan gravy. Cook for a few minutes, stirring frequently. If too much of the stock boils away before it combines with the drippings, add the remaining chicken stock, a tablespoon at a time, until the sauce tastes rich, but not too intense or too soupy. Taste for seasoning and add salt and pepper as needed. Pour over the chicken, or serve in a heated sauceboat.

Broiled Chicken

One secret to a succulent broiled chicken is to choose a bird that is young enough to be tender yet plump enough to be juicy. It may be called a broiler or a fryer or a fryer-broiler.

Serves 4

Ingredients
4 tablespoons butter
1 chicken, about 2½ to 3
    pounds, cut in quarters
1 teaspoon salt
Freshly ground pepper

Equipment
Small saucepan
Paper towels
Measuring spoons
Roasting pan with flat rack
Pastry brush
Oven mitts
Tongs
Bulb baster
Knife

1. Set an oven shelf about 6 inches from the source of heat and preheat the broiler to its highest setting.

2. In the small saucepan melt the butter over low heat and set aside while you prepare the chicken.

3. Wash the chicken thoroughly under cold water and pat dry with paper towels. Place the chicken skin side down on the flat rack on the roasting pan and sprinkle the exposed side with ½

teaspoon salt and a few grindings of pepper. With the pastry brush, brush about a tablespoon of melted butter over the chicken pieces.

4. Place the roasting pan under the preheated broiler.

5. While the chicken is beginning to broil, wash your hands and any utensils that touched the raw chicken in hot soapy water and dry well.

6. Wearing oven mitts, pull the broiler pan out and brush a little more melted butter over the chicken. Continue broiling for 10 minutes.

7. Again, pull the pan out (wear the oven mitts) and turn the chicken pieces over, using the tongs. Sprinkle with the remaining ½ teaspoon of salt and a few grindings of pepper. Brush with another tablespoon of melted butter. You should follow this basting procedure several times — turning the chicken over, brushing with melted butter, and broiling for 10 minutes — until the chicken is done, which takes about 35 minutes. If you run out of melted butter, baste the chicken pieces with pan drippings picked up with the bulb baster. Test the chicken by pricking the fattest

part of the thigh with the point of a knife. If the juice runs clear, the chicken is done; if not, broil another few minutes.

8. With the tongs transfer the chicken pieces to a heated platter and pour the pan drippings over them.

Baked Chicken

This is a crusty chicken, somewhere between broiled and southern fried, and easier to make than either of them.

Serves 4

Ingredients
1 tablespoon cooking oil
1 chicken, about 2½ to 3
   pounds, cut in quarters
1 teaspoon salt
Freshly ground pepper
2 tablespoons butter
½ cup seasoned bread
   crumbs

Equipment
Shallow baking dish, to hold
   the chicken pieces in
   one layer
Measuring spoons
Measuring cups
Paper towel
Aluminum foil
Knife
Small saucepan
Oven mitts
Rubber spatula

1. Preheat oven to 375°F.

2. Lightly oil the baking dish, using a paper towel to distribute the oil.

3. Wash the chicken thoroughly under cold water and pat dry with paper towels. Place the chicken skin side up in the pan in one layer and sprinkle with the salt and a few grindings of pep-

per. Cover the top tightly with a piece of aluminum foil and bake 30 to 45 minutes. The chicken is done when you prick the fattest part of the thigh with the point of a knife and the juice runs clear.

4. While the chicken is cooking, melt the butter in the small saucepan over low heat. Add the bread crumbs and stir. Set aside.

5. When the chicken is done, remove the baking pan, wearing the oven mitts, turn the oven off, and turn on the broiler to High.

6. Discard the foil covering and pat the buttered bread crumbs over the skin side of the chicken pieces with a rubber spatula. Slide the chicken under the broiler to brown the crumb topping for a few minutes. Watch closely so that the crumbs don't start to burn.

Microwaved Chicken Breasts

Boneless chicken breasts are marvelous for chicken salad and sandwiches and can be dressed up with any number of sauces. The microwave cooks them more quickly and easily than poaching or steaming, and without risk of their becoming rubbery or stringy. This recipe is for a large or medium-sized microwave oven, about 600 to 700 watts. If you have a smaller microwave, or are cooking a different amount of chicken, consult the microwave directions.

Makes 4 half breasts

Ingredients
2 boneless, skinless chicken
    breasts, about 10 ounces
    each

Equipment
Paper towels
Microwave-safe dinner plate
    or small dish
Microwave plastic wrap
Oven mitts
Knife

1. Rinse the breasts under cold water and dry with paper towels. Cut each breast in half and place them in a microwave-safe dish, with the thickest ends of each piece toward the outside.

2. Cover tightly with microwave plastic wrap and place in the microwave oven.

3. Cook on High for 5 minutes.

4. Take the dish out of the oven, wearing oven mitts. On the far side, away from your face, pierce the plastic wrap with the point of the knife to let the steam escape. Slowly and carefully open the plastic wrap on the side away from you and test the chicken for doneness. If it looks glassy or translucent when pierced with the knife, cover it and cook it another minute or two.

Panfried Fish

This is a quick and easy way to cook small whole fish, such as brook trout, sea bass, and mackerel, and boneless fillets. Count on about ½ pound of fish per person if the bones are not removed, or ⅓ pound filleted, boned fish.

Serves 4

Ingredients
4 small whole fish, heads
    and tails removed, or
    1½ pounds fillets
1½ teaspoons salt
Freshly ground pepper
⅓ to ½ cup flour or
    cornmeal
6 tablespoons (¾ stick)
    butter
2 tablespoons vegetable oil
1 lemon
2 tablespoons chopped
    parsley

Equipment
Serving platter
Measuring cups
Measuring spoons
Paper towels
Waxed paper
Large heavy cast-iron skillet
Wide spatula
Knife
Wooden spoon

1. Preheat the oven to the lowest setting (about 200–250°F.) and place the serving platter in it to warm.

2. Wash the fish in cold water and dry lightly with paper towels.

112

Sprinkle the salt over the fish and, if you are cooking whole fish, rub a little salt inside each cavity. Grind a little fresh pepper over each fish or fillet.

3. Spread the flour or cornmeal on a piece of waxed paper. Place one side of each fish or fillet on the flour or cornmeal, turn over to coat the other side, then shake off the excess. Repeat for the remaining fish.

4. In the skillet, melt the butter over high heat and add the oil. When the fats are hot and begin to brown, add the fish, lower the heat to medium, and panfry the fish on one side for 2 to 3 minutes. Using the wide spatula, turn each fish over carefully and panfry on the other side for 2 to 3 minutes. If the frying pan can't hold all the fish at the same time, fry two pieces at a time; you may need to add more butter and oil for the second batch. Using the spatula, carefully transfer the cooked fish to the heated serving platter.

5. Cut the lemon in half and squeeze the juice into the frying pan. Stir with the wooden spoon to incorporate the pan drippings and cook for a minute or two. Spoon the lemony pan juices over the fish on the serving platter, and sprinkle with chopped parsley.

Broiled Fish Steaks

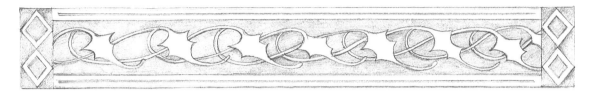

The best kinds of fish for broiling are fish steaks, cut between ½ and 1 inch thick. Thinner steaks and fillets are likely to dry out in the broiler and do better panfried (page 112) or microwaved (page 116). Figure about ⅓ pound of boneless steaks or ½ pound with the bone per person.

Serves 4

Ingredients

4 fish steaks, such as salmon or swordfish, ¾ inch thick
1 teaspoon salt
Freshly ground pepper
6 tablespoons (¾ stick) butter
1 tablespoon vegetable oil
1 tablespoon snipped dill or finely chopped parsley
1 lemon, quartered

Equipment

Roasting pan with flat rack
Measuring spoons
Paper towels
Small saucepan
Oven mitts
Pastry brush
Wide spatula
Small knife

1. Set the roasting pan and rack in the broiler, 3 or 4 inches from the source of heat, and preheat the broiler at its highest setting.

2. Rinse the fish steaks under cold water and pat dry with paper towels. Lightly sprinkle each side with the salt and a few grindings of pepper.

3. In the small saucepan melt the butter over low heat, and set aside.

4. Wearing the oven mitts, slide the hot broiler pan and rack out of the oven and, using the pastry brush, grease the rack with the vegetable oil. Lay the fish steaks on it, taking care not to touch the hot pan, and brush the tops of the fish steaks generously with some of the melted butter. Put the oven mitts back on and slide the pan and rack back under the broiler. Broil the fish for 5 minutes, brushing again with some melted butter after 2 to 3 minutes.

5. Wearing the mitts, slide the broiler pan and rack out of the oven and carefully turn the fish steaks over with a wide spatula. Brush the steaks with more of the melted butter and slide the pan and rack back under the broiler. Broil for 2 to 3 minutes, then test one of the steaks for doneness by making a small cut with the sharp knife. If the exposed flesh is opaque, no longer glassy and translucent, the steaks are done; if not, brush with more melted butter and broil another 1 to 3 minutes.

6. Transfer the fish steaks to a heated serving platter, pour the pan drippings and any remaining melted butter over them, sprinkle with the dill or parsley, and garnish with the lemon quarters.

Microwaved Fish

Moist heat is a delicious way to cook most fish, and the traditional way of doing it was by poaching or braising. The microwave does the job more quickly and easily and produces wonderfully tender fish. You can microwave all cuts and kinds of fish — fillets, steaks, whole fish — but the exact timing depends on the thickness and weight of the fish, on the number of pieces you cook at the same time, and on the wattage of your microwave. This recipe is for a large or medium-sized microwave oven, about 600 to 700 watts; if you have a smaller microwave, consult the microwave directions.

Serves 4

Ingredients	Equipment
4 fillets or fish steaks	Measuring spoons
1 teaspoon salt	Paper towels
Freshly ground pepper	Microwave-safe dish
1 lemon, quartered	Microwave plastic wrap
	Small knife
	Wide spatula
	Oven mitts

1. Rinse the fillets or steaks under cold water and dry with paper towels. Place them in a microwave-safe dish, with the thickest ends of each piece toward the outside.

2. Lightly sprinkle them with ½ teaspoon of the salt and a few

grindings of pepper, then turn over each piece and season with the remaining salt and more pepper. Cover tightly with microwave plastic wrap and place in the microwave oven.

3. Cook ½-inch-thick fillets or steaks on High for 5 minutes, and 1-inch-thick fillets or steaks on High for 6 minutes. If your oven doesn't have a turntable or emit its microwaves in a rotating pattern, turn the cooking dish 90 degrees (a quarter of a circle) halfway through the cooking time.

4. Wearing oven mitts, take the dish out of the oven, and on the far side, away from your face, pierce the plastic wrap with the point of the knife to let the steam escape. Slowly and carefully open the plastic wrap on the side away from you, and test the fish for doneness. If it isn't opaque all through when pierced with the small knife, cover it and cook it another minute or two.

5. With the wide spatula transfer the fish to a heated serving platter and serve with the lemon quarters.

Vegetables

Asparagus

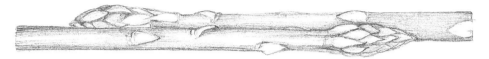

Buy asparagus spears of the same thickness so they all cook evenly, and look for tightly closed tips. You can serve them hot with melted butter, or at room temperature with Vinaigrette Dressing (page 189) or hollandaise sauce.

Serves 4

Ingredients
24 stalks asparagus

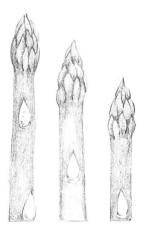

Equipment
Cutting board
Small knife
Vegetable peeler
To steam:
Large pot with lid
Steamer basket
Tongs
To microwave:
Rectangular microwave-safe
    dish
Microwave plastic wrap
Oven mitts

1. Wash the asparagus stalks carefully to remove any sand from the tips. Lay them on a cutting board and remove the pale woody bottoms with the small knife, cutting the stalks to a uniform length. With the vegetable peeler, peel each stalk, starting just below the tip and working down.

2. *To steam:* Fill a pot large enough to hold them with an inch or two of water, fit a steamer rack on or in it (depending on your equipment), and bring the water to a boil. With tongs, place the asparagus spears in the steamer in several layers, cover the pot, and lower the heat to moderate. After 6 minutes test the spears with the tip of the knife; the spears should be crisp-tender but not soft. Continue steaming until done, testing every couple of minutes.

3. *To microwave:* Arrange the stalks in two or three layers in a microwave-safe dish just big enough to hold them, with all the tips pointing in the same direction, and cover tightly with microwave plastic wrap. Cook at High for 7 to 9 minutes, depending on the thickness of the spears; fewer and/or thinner asparagus takes less time to cook. Take the dish out of the oven and on the far side, away from your face, pierce the plastic wrap with the point of the knife to let the steam escape. Slowly and carefully open the plastic wrap on the side away from you and test for doneness. Re-cover and cook another minute or two, if necessary.

Broccoli and Cauliflower

The trick to cooking good broccoli and cauliflower is to cook them only until they are crisp-tender and, in the case of broccoli, still bright green. Serve these vegetables hot with melted butter or hollandaise sauce.

Serves 3 to 4

Ingredients
1 pound broccoli or 1
   medium head
   cauliflower

Equipment
Knife
Vegetable peeler
To steam:
Large pot with lid
Steamer basket
To microwave:
Microwave-safe dish
Plastic wrap
Oven mitts

1. Wash the broccoli and cut away the thick tough stems and outer leaves. Divide the head into serving-sized portions. Peel the stems lightly with the vegetable peeler and pierce the thickest stems lightly with the point of the knife. For the cauliflower, wash the head well, remove the outer thick green leaves, cut off the stalk, and break off the florets.

2. *To steam:* Place the steamer basket in the pot and pour an inch

or two of water in below the bottom of the steamer. Bring the water to a boil and arrange the broccoli or cauliflower pieces in the basket. Cover and steam about 5 minutes, then pierce the broccoli stems or the cauliflower florets with the point of a knife to test for doneness. They should be just tender but not soft. If not, cook a little bit longer — but no more than a minute or so. Be careful not to overcook!

3. *To microwave:* Arrange the prepared broccoli or cauliflower in a microwave-safe dish with the stems pointing out, sprinkle with water, and cover tightly with plastic wrap. Cook on High for about 7 to 9 minutes. If your oven doesn't have a turntable or emit its microwaves in a rotating pattern, turn the dish 90 degrees halfway through the cooking time (wear your oven mitts). Take the dish out of the oven and on the far side, away from your face, pierce the plastic wrap with the point of a knife to let the steam escape. Slowly and carefully open the plastic wrap on the side away from you.

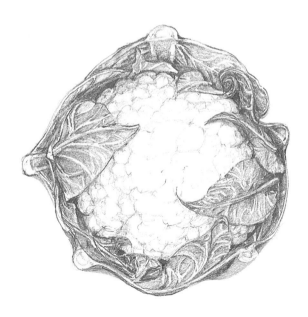

Carrots

Young carrots are especially delicious when cooked simply, like this. They're also wonderfully versatile — we use them in Carrot Cake (page 203) and Chilled Carrot Soup (page 50).

Serves 4

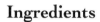

Ingredients	Equipment
1 pound carrots	Cutting board
2 tablespoons butter	Small knife
Salt	Vegetable peeler
Freshly ground pepper	*To steam:*
Freshly grated nutmeg	2-quart saucepan with lid
	Steamer basket
	To microwave:
	Microwave-safe dish
	Microwave plastic wrap
	Oven mitts

1. Cut off the leaves and scrape the skins with a vegetable peeler. Slice the carrots ¼ inch thick.

2. *To boil:* Put the slices in the saucepan, pour in boiling water to cover them, and cook, covered, over medium heat about 8 to 10 minutes.

3. *To steam:* Fill the saucepan with an inch or two of water, fit

the steamer basket in it, and bring the water to a boil. Put the sliced carrots in the basket, cover, and steam about 10 minutes.

4. *To microwave:* Arrange the slices in layers in a microwave-safe dish just big enough to hold them, cover tightly with plastic wrap, and cook about 6 minutes. If your oven doesn't have a turntable or emit its microwaves in a rotating pattern, turn the dish 90 degrees halfway through the cooking time, wearing oven mitts. Take the dish out of the oven and on the far side, away from your face, pierce the plastic wrap with the point of a knife to let the steam escape. Slowly and carefully open the plastic wrap on the side away from you and test for doneness. They should be crisp-tender. Re-cover and cook another minute or two, if necessary.

5. Drain the cooked carrots. Toss them with the butter and season with salt, pepper, and a few grains of nutmeg.

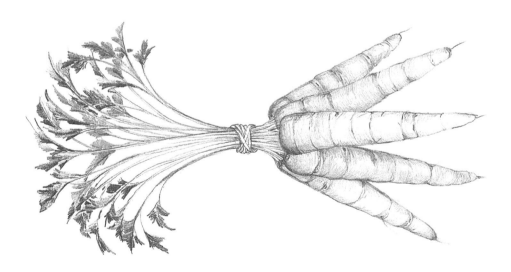

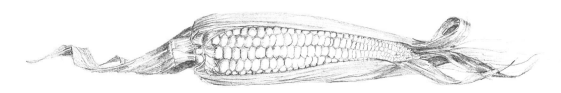

Corn on the Cob

Fresh-picked is the key to great corn, and you're lucky if you can get it at a local farm or vegetable stand. Figure at least two ears of corn per person.

Serves 4

Ingredients	**Equipment**
8 ears fresh corn	Large kettle or pot
1 teaspoon sugar	Measuring spoons
Softened butter	Small knife
Salt	Tongs

1. Fill the kettle ⅔ full with water and bring it to a boil.

2. Meanwhile, remove the husks and silky threads from the ears of corn. Don't husk the corn until you're ready to cook it.

3. When the water is boiling, add the sugar and the corn. When the water comes to a boil again, cook for 5 minutes, or until the kernels are tender when you test them with the point of the small knife.

4. Using the tongs, transfer the cooked ears of corn to a platter and serve at once with softened butter and salt.

Green Beans

Young, small beans are best, but whatever their size, look for firm crisp beans of fresh color that snap when you break them. Serve them as an appetizer with a favorite dip, in a green salad, or, sprinkled with dill and tossed with French or Vinaigrette Dressing (page 189), as a salad themselves.

Serves 4

Ingredients
1 pound green beans
2 tablespoons butter
Salt
¼ cup toasted slivered
    almonds (optional)

Equipment
Small knife
Large pot
Colander
Steamer basket
2-quart saucepan
Measuring cups (optional)

1. Wash the beans and cut off the stem ends. Leave them whole, or cut very large beans in half.

2. Bring water in the large pot to a boil, add the beans, and cook, uncovered, about 5 to 10 minutes, or until they are crisp-tender and still crunchy. Drain through the colander and rinse briefly with cold water to stop the cooking.

3. *To steam:* Place the steamer basket in a pot and pour an inch or two of water in below the bottom of the basket. Bring the

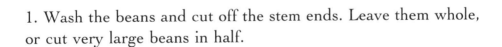

water to a boil and arrange the beans in the basket. Cover and steam about 10 minutes, then pierce a bean with the point of the knife to test for doneness. It should be still crisp. Continue to cook, testing every couple of minutes until done, but be careful not to overcook.

4. In the saucepan melt the butter over low heat, add the beans, and toss. Season with salt and sprinkle with toasted almonds, if desired.

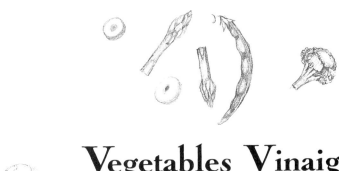

Vegetables Vinaigrette

A colorful variety of crisp cooked vegetables marinated in a vinaigrette dressing is a lovely accompaniment to roasted, grilled, and poached meats and fish, especially in warm weather. You can use practically any combination of asparagus, broccoli florets, thin carrot rounds, cauliflower florets, corn kernels, or green beans.

Serves 4

Ingredients
4 cups mixed cooked
    vegetables
1 recipe (½ cup) French or
    Vinaigrette Dressing
    (page 189)

Equipment
Large mixing bowl

1. In the large mixing bowl toss the cooked vegetables in the vinaigrette dressing and refrigerate until ready to serve.

Broiled Tomatoes

These are delicious with fish and roasted or grilled meats, and they look beautiful on the plate.

Serves 4

Ingredients

4 ripe, firm tomatoes, 2 to 3 inches in diameter
1 teaspoon salt
Freshly ground black pepper
4 tablespoons fresh bread crumbs
4 tablespoons freshly grated Parmesan cheese
2 tablespoons butter

Equipment

Knife
Cutting board
Measuring spoons
Shallow baking pan
Small mixing bowl
Oven mitts
Spatula

1. Set the oven rack about 4 to 5 inches below the broiler unit, then preheat the broiler.

2. Cut the tomatoes in half crosswise and place them in the baking pan, cut sides up. Sprinkle with salt and a few grindings of pepper.

3. In a small bowl, combine the bread crumbs and Parmesan cheese and divide the mixture evenly over the tops of the tomatoes. Cut the butter into bits and dot the tops.

4. Broil the tomatoes 6 to 8 minutes, watching them carefully. If you see any signs of burning, lower the rack, with oven mitts on. When the topping is golden and the tomatoes are still firm, transfer the baking pan, wearing the mitts, from the oven to a heatproof counter or stove top. With the spatula, put the tomato halves on a heated serving platter.

Stir-Fried Vegetables

Stir-frying is a way to sauté vegetables very quickly so they keep their flavor, color, and crispness. The technique, which comes from the Chinese, uses a small amount of oil and goes so fast you must have all your ingredients prepared and at hand.

Stir-Fried Asparagus

Serves 4

Ingredients
1½ pounds asparagus
¼ cup chicken stock or
    water
2 tablespoons vegetable oil
Salt
Freshly ground pepper

Equipment
Measuring spoons
Measuring cups
Cutting board
Knife
Paper towels
Vegetable peeler
1-quart saucepan with lid
Wok or 10-inch sauté pan or
    12-inch skillet with lid
Oven mitts
Wooden spoon
Slotted spoon

1. Wash the asparagus carefully to remove any sand from the tips. Lay the stalks on the cutting board and cut off the pale woody bottoms; the stalks need not be the same length. Cut off the tips and set them aside on a paper towel. With a vegetable peeler, peel each stalk. Cut each stalk on the diagonal into ½-

132

inch-long pieces with slanted ends, and set them aside on paper towels to be sure they are dry.

2. In the small saucepan bring the chicken stock or water to a boil, remove from heat, cover, and set aside.

3. Heat the oil in the wok or sauté pan over high heat. When you see watery ripples in the oil, put on the oven mitts and tip the pan from side to side to oil the entire surface. Drop the asparagus stalks into the pan and toss them with a wooden spoon until all the pieces are coated with oil, about 1 minute. Then add the tips and gently toss them in the same way for another minute.

4. Pour the hot stock into the pan and stir gently until it comes to a boil. Reduce heat to moderate and cook for another 2 to 3 minutes, until the asparagus is crisp-tender. With the slotted spoon transfer the asparagus to a warmed bowl. Season to taste with salt and pepper and serve at once.

Stir-Fried Beans

Serves 4

Ingredients
1 pound young green beans
¼ cup chicken stock or
    water
2 tablespoons vegetable oil
Salt
Freshly ground pepper

Equipment
Measuring spoons
Measuring cups
Cutting board
Small knife
Paper towels
1-quart saucepan with lid
Wok or 10-inch sauté pan or
    12-inch skillet with lid
Oven mitts
Wooden spoon
Slotted spoon

133

1. Trim the beans at each end, put them on the cutting board, and cut them on the diagonal into 2-inch-long pieces. Wash the beans, pat them dry with a paper towel, and set them aside.

2. In the saucepan bring the chicken stock or water to a boil, remove from heat, cover, and set aside.

3. Heat the oil in the wok or sauté pan over high heat. When you see watery ripples in the oil, put on the oven mitts and tip the pan from side to side to oil the entire surface. Drop the beans into the pan and toss them with a wooden spoon until all the pieces are coated with oil, about 2 minutes.

4. Pour the hot stock into the pan and stir gently until it comes to a boil. Reduce heat to moderate and cook for another 2 to 3 minutes, until the beans are crisp-tender. With the slotted spoon transfer the beans to a warmed bowl. Season to taste with salt and pepper and serve at once.

Stir-Fried Broccoli

Serves 4

Ingredients
1 bunch broccoli (about 1½ pounds)
¼ cup chicken stock or water
2 tablespoons vegetable oil
Salt
Freshly ground pepper

Equipment
Measuring spoons
Measuring cups
Cutting board
Small knife
Paper towels
1-quart saucepan with lid
Wok or 10-inch sauté pan or 12-inch skillet with lid
Oven mitts
Wooden spoon
Slotted spoon

1. Wash the broccoli and lay it on the cutting board. Cut the florets and an inch or so of their stems from the thick stalks. If the florets are large, divide them into half or thirds, from the stem up. Pat them dry with paper towels and set them aside. With the small sharp knife peel the tough skin and any leaves from the remaining thick stems. Cut them diagonally into ½-inch sections with slanted ends and pat them dry with paper towels.

2. In the small saucepan bring the chicken stock or water to a boil, remove from heat, cover, and set aside.

3. Heat the oil in the wok or pan over high heat. When you see watery ripples in the oil, put oven mitts on and tip the pan from side to side to oil the entire surface. Drop the stem pieces into the pan and toss with a wooden spoon until they are all coated with oil, about 1 minute. Then add the florets and gently toss them in the same way for another minute.

4. Pour the hot stock into the pan and stir gently until it comes to a boil. Reduce heat to moderate and cook for another 4 to 5 minutes, or until the stalks are crisp-tender. With the slotted spoon transfer the broccoli to a warmed bowl. Season to taste with salt and pepper and serve at once.

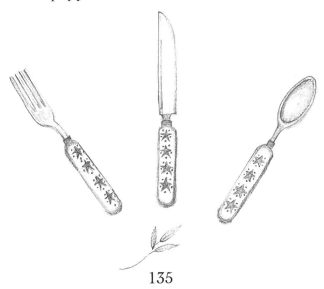

Ratatouille

This mix of several vegetables is wonderful for a crowd. It's delicious hot or cold, and it keeps for at least a week in the refrigerator and for several months in the freezer.

Makes 3 quarts, or 12 to 16 servings

Ingredients

2 medium eggplants (about 2½ pounds)
2 teaspoons salt
3 medium zucchini (about 1 pound)
2 green peppers
¼ cup olive oil
3 medium onions
2 garlic cloves, peeled
2 28-ounce cans plum tomatoes, coarsely chopped
1 teaspoon sugar
1 cup chopped fresh parsley
1 cup chopped fresh basil, if available
Freshly ground pepper

Equipment

Measuring spoons
Measuring cups
Cutting board
Vegetable peeler
Medium knife
2 large mixing bowls
Heavy 5- or 6-quart cast-iron casserole
Garlic press
Wooden spoon
Colander
Oven mitts

136

1. Peel the eggplants with the vegetable peeler and cut them into 1-inch cubes with the medium knife on the cutting board. Put the pieces into one large mixing bowl, sprinkle them with the salt, and let sit.

2. Wash the zucchini and slice them ½ inch thick. Put into the other bowl. Core and seed the green peppers and cut them into ½-inch pieces. Add them to the zucchini slices.

3. Preheat the oven to 350°F.

4. Heat the olive oil in the heavy casserole over medium heat.

5. Meanwhile, peel and slice the onions. When the oil is heated, add the onions and the garlic that has been mashed through a garlic press. Sauté over medium heat for about 5 minutes, stirring occasionally with the wooden spoon until the onions are golden but not brown. Add the zucchini and green pepper and sauté 3 minutes, stirring occasionally.

6. Drain the eggplants through the colander, add them to the casserole, and sauté for 3 minutes, stirring occasionally.

7. Stir in the canned tomatoes, sugar, and ¾ cup of the fresh parsley and ¾ cup of the basil. Cook 10 minutes.

8. With oven mitts on, carefully transfer the casserole to the oven and bake 30 minutes, uncovered. Taste for seasoning and add more salt and freshly ground pepper, if needed. Before serving, sprinkle the remaining ¼ cup parsley and ¼ cup basil over the top.

9. If you're not going to serve the ratatouille right away, cool it a little before refrigerating. Store the remaining fresh parsley and basil in small plastic bags in the refrigerator until ready to use.

Baked Potatoes

Use firm, smooth Idaho potatoes with no blemishes. New potatoes don't bake well, and "all-purpose" potatoes get mealy. Pick potatoes of uniform size for best results.

Ingredients
1 potato per person
Butter
Salt

Equipment
Vegetable brush
Paper towels
Small knife
Oven mitts

1. Preheat the oven to 450°F.

2. Scrub the potatoes with the vegetable brush under running water, then dry with a paper towel. Don't follow the popular custom of wrapping potatoes in foil because that retains the steam and prevents them from becoming nice and flaky. Place the clean potatoes directly on a rack in the center of the oven individually or in a shallow pan (which makes it easier to take them out). Bake for 40 minutes to 1 hour, depending on size. To test, pull out the rack or baking pan, wearing oven mitts, pick up a potato in a folded paper towel, and squeeze it gently; if it feels soft, the potatoes are done.

3. Cut a cross in the top of each potato and press the sides so that steam will escape. Serve with butter and salt.

4. You can "bake" potatoes in the microwave if you're in a hurry, but they will taste more steamed than flaky. To microwave, prick the top of each clean potato several times with a fork, and place on paper towels in the microwave oven. Cook up to four potatoes at a time on High: 7 minutes for 1 potato, 11 minutes for 2, 15 minutes for 3, 19 minutes for 4.

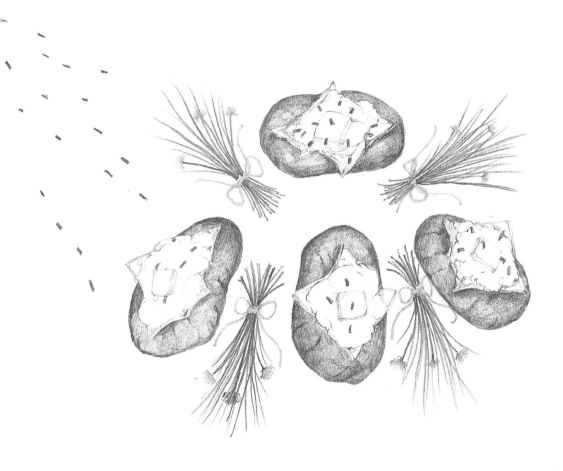

Boiled New Potatoes

New potatoes are simply young potatoes and don't need to be peeled for cooking or eating. They are delicious served in their skins, plain or lightly salted.

Serves 4

Ingredients
1 tablespoon salt
12 small new potatoes of
    uniform size

Equipment
Large pot
Measuring spoons
Vegetable brush
Cake tester or fork
Colander

1. Pour 3 quarts of water into the large pot, add the salt, and bring to a boil.

2. Meanwhile, scrub the potatoes well under running water with the vegetable brush. Drop them in the pot, lower the heat to moderate, and boil them for 15 to 20 minutes, or until a test potato feels tender when pierced with a fork or cake tester. Place the colander in the sink and carefully drain the potatoes. Serve at once, plain or lightly salted.

Parsley New Potatoes

Serves 4

Ingredients
1 tablespoon salt
12 small new potatoes of
    uniform size
8 tablespoons (1 stick)
    butter
¼ cup finely chopped parsley
½ fresh lemon, cut into 4
    wedges

Equipment
Large pot
Measuring spoons
Measuring cups
Vegetable brush
Cake tester or fork
Colander
12-inch skillet

1. Pour 3 quarts of water into the large pot, add the salt, and bring to a boil.

2. Meanwhile, scrub the potatoes well under running water with the vegetable brush. Drop them in the pot, lower the heat to moderate, and boil for 15 to 20 minutes, or until a test potato feels tender when pierced with the fork or cake tester. Place the colander in the sink and carefully drain the potatoes.

3. Melt the butter in the skillet and add the cooked potatoes, shaking the pan until each potato is well coated. Sprinkle with parsley and serve with lemon wedges on the side.

Variation

Mint New Potatoes: Substitute freshly cut mint leaves for the parsley and follow the same recipe.

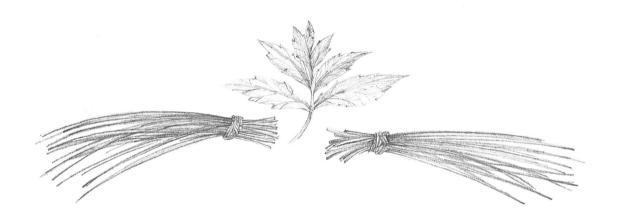

Mashed Potatoes

Serves 4

Ingredients

1 tablespoon salt
2 pounds all-purpose
    potatoes (about 5
    medium) of uniform size
⅓ cup milk
3 tablespoons butter,
    softened
Salt
Freshly ground pepper

Equipment

Large pot
Measuring spoons
Measuring cups
Vegetable brush
Vegetable peeler
Cake tester or fork
1-quart saucepan or 2-cup
    glass measuring cup
Large mixing bowl
Colander
Small knife
Potato masher
Wooden spoon
Whisk or electric mixer
    (optional)

1. Pour 3 quarts of water into the large pot, add the salt, and bring to a boil.

2. Meanwhile, scrub the potatoes well under running water with the vegetable brush. Remove the skins with the vegetable peeler. If potatoes are very large, cut them into uniform-sized pieces

(halves or quarters) so they cook at the same pace. Drop them in the pot, lower the heat to moderate, and, depending on size, boil for about 20 to 30 minutes, or until a potato feels tender when pierced with the fork or cake tester.

3. Heat the milk slowly on the stove in the saucepan over low heat, or heat it in the microwave in the glass measuring cup, tightly covered, for 45 seconds on High.

4. Warm the mixing bowl by filling it with hot water, then drain and dry it.

5. Drain the potatoes through the colander in the sink. Cut them into quarters with the small knife and put them in the heated mixing bowl. Mash them with the potato masher, working out as many of the lumps as you can. With the wooden spoon, beat in the softened butter, a tablespoon at a time, then slowly pour in the hot milk, still beating with the spoon. If you want fluffier potatoes, whip them with the whisk or electric mixer.

6. Taste for seasoning and add salt and freshly ground pepper, if needed. Pile on a heated serving dish and serve at once.

Candied Sweet Potatoes

Sweet potatoes make healthy and delicious eating, and this particular recipe is so good, don't wait for a holiday meal to make it.

Serves 4

Ingredients
4 medium sweet potatoes or
    yams
1 teaspoon salt
4 tablespoons (½ stick)
    butter
½ cup brown sugar
¼ cup water

Equipment
Large pot
Vegetable brush
Measuring spoons
Measuring cups
Cake tester or fork
Colander
Cutting board
Small knife
Heavy 12-inch skillet with
    lid
Wooden spoon

1. In the large pot bring 3 quarts of water to a boil.

2. Meanwhile, scrub the potatoes well under running water with the vegetable brush. Drop them in the pot, add the salt, lower the heat to moderate, and boil for 15 to 20 minutes, or until a test potato feels tender when pierced with the fork or cake tester. Drain the potatoes through the colander in the sink.

3. When the potatoes are cool enough to handle, peel them with the small knife. On the cutting board, cut small potatoes in half lengthwise and large ones into ½-inch slices crosswise; the shapes don't have to be uniform.

4. In the skillet melt the butter with the brown sugar over moderate heat, add the potatoes, and turn them with a wooden spoon until they are well coated and slightly brown. Add the water and cover the pan. Reduce the heat to low and cook until the potatoes are glazed, about 10 to 15 minutes. From time to time, uncover the pan and spoon some of the syrup over the potatoes.

Pastas and Grains

Pasta comes in dozens of shapes and sizes, from long thin rods of spaghetti and thicker tubes of macaroni to tiny rice-sized orzo and corkscrew-shaped rotelle. There are wide flat pastas to layer into a lasagna, large tubes and shells to stuff, tiny dots to put in soups, complicated shapes to catch thick sauces.

They are all made of flour and water, sometimes enriched with eggs, occasionally flavored with spinach, tomatoes, or other vegetables, which gives them a golden, green, or rosy tint. Most pastas are dried and sold in boxes or in cellophane packages; sometimes in a specialty food store you can find fresh pasta, which must be refrigerated and cooks in just a minute or two.

Basic Pasta

All dried pastas are cooked the same way, but the length of time depends on size and shape. Fine, small shapes cook much more quickly than large, dense pieces. Use the recommended cooking time on the box of pasta only as a general guide (it's usually too long); start testing your pasta several minutes earlier.

Serves 4

Ingredients
1 tablespoon salt
1 pound dried pasta

Equipment
Large pot
Measuring spoons
Tongs
Serving dish
Colander

1. Pour 8 quarts of water into the large pot, add the salt, and bring to a full boil. Gently add the pasta so as not to disturb the boil; with long pieces like spaghetti and noodles, dip the ends into the boiling water and, as they soften, coil the lengths into the pot.

2. Boil rapidly until the pasta is tender but firm, what the Italians call *al dente*. As a rough guide, cooking time for a pound of fine angel hair is about 3 to 5 minutes, for spaghetti about 6 to 9 minutes, and for medium shells about 12 to 15 minutes. With tongs, grasp a strand or a small piece a minute or two before you

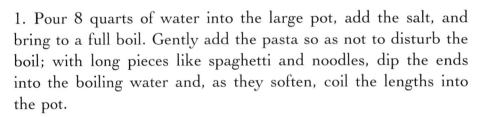
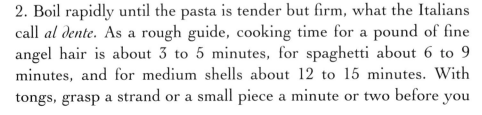

think it will be done; it should taste a little chewy but not hard, and you shouldn't see any white uncooked dough in the center. If it needs more cooking, test every minute so it doesn't get overdone and mushy.

3. Meanwhile, heat the serving dish by running very hot water over it, then dry it.

4. Put a colander in the sink and drain the cooked pasta into it. Pour the drained pasta back into the cooking pot. If you are going to serve the pasta already mixed with a sauce, add the sauce now to the pot and mix together, then transfer the sauced pasta to the warm serving dish and serve at once. If you are going to serve the pasta separately at the table, first drizzle a tablespoon or two of olive oil over the drained pasta to keep it from sticking together, and toss well. Then transfer the pasta to the heated serving dish and serve at once, with a bowl of the sauce on the side.

TYPE OF PASTA	COOKING TIME
Angel hair	3 to 5 minutes
Spaghetti	6 to 9 minutes
Medium shells	12 to 15 minutes

Tomato Sauce

This is an all-purpose tomato sauce. You can make it ahead and freeze it or refrigerate it, then reheat it when needed.

Makes about 4 cups; serves 4 to 6

Ingredients
3 tablespoons olive oil
1 clove garlic, peeled
2 onions, peeled and
    chopped
1 28-ounce can Italian-style
    tomatoes
1 12-ounce can tomato paste
1 cup tomato juice
1 tablespoon sugar
1 tablespoon fresh minced
    basil or 2 teaspoons
    dried basil
Salt
Freshly ground pepper

Equipment
Measuring cups
Measuring spoons
4-quart saucepan
Garlic press
Knife
Wooden spoon

1. Heat the oil in the saucepan.

2. Press the garlic through the garlic press into the pan, add the chopped onions, and cook over moderate heat until the onions are translucent. Add the tomatoes, cutting large pieces in half

150

with the knife. Stir in the tomato paste, tomato juice, and sugar with the wooden spoon. Lower the heat and simmer 1½ hours, uncovered. If the sauce gets too thick, stir in a little water, up to ¼ cup, but don't thin the sauce too much.

3. Add the basil and season to taste with salt and freshly ground pepper. Continue cooking over low heat 15 more minutes, or until the sauce is nice and thick.

4. Spoon the sauce over freshly cooked pasta on a heated platter.

Meat Sauce

Makes 5 cups; serves 4 to 6

Ingredients

3 tablespoons olive oil
1 clove garlic, peeled
2 onions, peeled and
    chopped
1 pound ground beef
1 28-ounce can Italian-style
    tomatoes
1 12-ounce can tomato paste
1 cup tomato juice
1 tablespoon sugar
1 tablespoon fresh minced
    basil or 2 teaspoons
    dried basil
Salt
Freshly ground pepper

Equipment

Measuring spoons
Measuring cups
Heavy 4-quart saucepan
Garlic press
Wooden spoon
Bulb baster or large spoon
Knife

1. Heat the oil in the saucepan.

2. Press the garlic through the garlic press into the pan, add the chopped onions, and cook over moderate heat until the onions are translucent.

3. Add the ground beef, stirring with a wooden spoon to break up the meat into small pieces. Cook over medium heat until the meat loses its pinkness. Remove the fat with the spoon or bulb baster and discard.

4. Add the tomatoes; cut large pieces in half with the knife. Stir in the tomato paste, tomato juice, and sugar. Lower the heat and simmer 1½ hours, uncovered. If the sauce gets too thick, stir in a little water, up to ¼ cup, but don't thin the sauce too much.

5. Add the basil and season to taste with salt and freshly ground pepper. Continue cooking over low heat 15 minutes more, or until the sauce is nice and thick.

6. Spoon the sauce over freshly cooked pasta on a heated platter.

Meat Balls in Tomato Sauce

Serves 4 to 6

Ingredients

1 egg
1 pound lean ground beef
½ cup seasoned bread
    crumbs
2 tablespoons milk
2 tablespoons snipped fresh
    basil or 2 teaspoons
    dried basil
¼ cup finely chopped fresh
    parsley
½ teaspoon salt
¼ teaspoon freshly ground
    pepper
2 tablespoons oil
4 cups (1 recipe) Tomato
    Sauce (page 150)
Freshly grated Parmesan
    cheese (optional)

Equipment

Measuring cups
Measuring spoons
Large mixing bowl
Fork
Waxed paper
Heavy 12-inch skillet with
    lid
Wooden spoon
Bulb baster or large spoon

1. In the mixing bowl beat the egg lightly with the fork. Add the ground beef, bread crumbs, milk, basil, parsley, salt, and pepper. Using your hands, combine the ingredients well. Shape into balls

1 to 1½ inches in diameter. As you make them, set them aside on a sheet of waxed paper.

2. In the skillet, heat the oil over medium heat. Add the meatballs and, using the wooden spoon, turn them on all sides to brown slightly. Remove excess fat with the bulb baster or spoon.

3. Add the tomato sauce, cover, and simmer over low heat for 30 minutes.

4. Spoon over freshly cooked pasta on a heated platter. Sprinkle with Parmesan cheese, if desired.

Pesto

This is more of a puree than a sauce; it is made from fresh basil and is really easy to make. It's marvelous over pasta, and you can also spoon it over minestrone or spread it on tomato halves and broil. Make lots of it in the summer when you can get fresh basil leaves. It freezes beautifully, so double or triple this recipe, put it into small jars (empty baby food jars work well), cover with a thin film of olive oil, cap them tightly, and freeze.

For 1 pound of pasta; serves 4

Ingredients
2 cloves garlic
2 cups fresh basil leaves, washed and dried
¼ cup pine nuts (pignoli) or shelled walnuts
½ teaspoon salt
¼ to ½ cup olive oil

Equipment
Measuring cups
Measuring spoons
Food processor

1. Remove the skin from the garlic cloves and chop them in the food processor. Add the basil leaves, nuts, and salt and process until the basil is finely chopped.

2. While processing, gradually add 3 tablespoons of the olive oil through the top opening. If the pesto is too thick, slowly add more olive oil until it's the desired consistency, up to another ¼ cup or so. Some people like a dense pesto puree, others an oilier, more liquid sauce.

Pasta Primavera

The combination of pasta and vegetables is delicious and definitely healthy. You can use all of these vegetables, or just a couple of them, or substitute other favorites; it doesn't matter which vegetables you use as long as you cook them only until they are crisp-tender.

Serves 6

Ingredients

1 bunch broccoli
2 medium zucchini
2 carrots
¼ pound fresh green beans
6-ounce package mushrooms
1 medium onion
½ cup vegetable oil
1 pint cherry tomatoes
1 pound pasta (spaghetti, capellini, or fettucine)
¼ cup chicken stock
½ cup freshly grated Parmesan cheese
¼ cup chopped fresh basil or ¼ cup chopped fresh parsley
Salt
Freshly ground pepper

Equipment

Measuring cups
6 small bowls or plates for the vegetables
Small knife
Vegetable peeler
Cutting board
Paper towels
4-quart saucepan with lid
Steamer basket
Oven mitts
Large mixing bowl
Heavy 12-inch iron skillet
Wooden spoon
Large pot
Colander
Tongs or two large kitchen forks

1. Prepare the vegetables and keep them in separate bowls until after you cook them. Cut off the broccoli florets and reserve the stems for another use. Peel the zucchini with the vegetable peeler. On the cutting board, cut them into quarters lengthwise and cut the quarters crosswise into ½-inch pieces. Scrape the carrots with the vegetable peeler and on the cutting board cut them into quarters lengthwise, then cut the quarters crosswise into ½-inch pieces. Trim the beans and cut them into 1-inch pieces. Wipe the mushrooms with paper towels and slice thin. Peel and finely chop the onion.

2. Pour an inch or two of water into the saucepan, set the steamer basket in the bottom, and bring the water to a boil. Add the broccoli florets to the steamer basket, cover, and steam over the boiling water only until they are crisp-tender, about 2 to 3 minutes. Wearing oven mitts, remove the steamer basket, carry it to the sink, and pour a little cold water over the broccoli to stop the cooking. Put the cooked broccoli in the large mixing bowl.

3. Repeat the same steaming process for the zucchini, carrots, and green beans, cooking each separately, draining, rinsing in cold water, then adding them to the mixing bowl. They will each take about 2 to 3 minutes to cook.

4. In the heavy skillet, heat 1 tablespoon of the vegetable oil and sauté the sliced mushrooms for about 5 minutes, occasionally shaking the pan. Transfer them to the mixing bowl.

5. Heat 3 more tablespoons of vegetable oil in the skillet and sauté the chopped onions over low heat until they are translucent, about 5 minutes, stirring occasionally with the wooden spoon. Add the cherry tomatoes and sauté another 3 to 5 minutes, shaking the skillet so they cook on all sides. Set the skillet aside.

6. In the large pot bring 8 quarts of water to a boil, and cook the pasta (see Basic Pasta, page 148).

7. While the pasta is cooking, add the chicken stock and remaining ¼ cup vegetable oil to the onions and tomatoes in the skillet. Stir in the vegetables from the mixing bowl. Set the skillet over low heat on the stove to heat the vegetables.

8. When the pasta has finished cooking, carefully carry the pot to the sink, wearing oven mitts, and drain it through the colander. Pour the drained pasta back into the cooking pot.

9. Add the hot vegetables to the pasta in the pot and toss them together, using tongs or two large kitchen forks. Add the Parmesan cheese and the chopped basil or parsley and toss again. Taste for seasoning and add salt and freshly ground pepper, if desired.

10. Transfer to a warm serving platter and serve with additional grated Parmesan cheese, if desired.

Lasagna

Lasagna is a wonderful dish for a lot of people. You can assemble it ahead, and refrigerate it, then bake it an hour before you're ready to serve it. Several hours before you're planning to use it, take it out of the refrigerator and let it come to room tempereature; it takes a surprisingly long time to heat through.

Serves 6 to 8

Ingredients

1 egg

2 cups (15-ounce container) ricotta cheese

¼ cup chopped fresh parsley

1 teaspoon salt

1 teaspoon freshly ground pepper

1 pound lasagna noodles

1 tablespoon olive oil

1 recipe (about 5 cups) Meat Sauce (page 152) or Tomato Sauce (page 150)

½ pound mozzarella cheese, grated

⅓ to ½ cup freshly grated Parmesan cheese (optional)

Equipment

Measuring cups

Measuring spoons

Large mixing bowl

Whisk

Large spoon

Large pot

Oven mitts

Colander

Large rectangular baking dish, about 9 × 13 × 3 inches

1. Break the egg into the mixing bowl and beat lightly with the whisk. Add the ricotta cheese, parsley, salt, and freshly ground pepper and combine well with the large spoon. Set aside.

2. In the large pot bring 8 quarts of water to a boil. Slowly add the lasagna noodles, a few at a time, and cook 8 to 10 minutes, or until they are tender but firm, *al dente*. You probably won't use all the noodles, but cook the whole amount because some strips will break, and some may stick to the bottom of the pot.

3. Wearing oven mitts, carefully carry the pot to the sink and add cold water to stop the cooking. As soon as the pot is cool enough to handle, pour out as much water as you can, still keeping the noodles in the pot. Add more cold water to cover the noodles, and add the olive oil to prevent them from sticking together. When you're ready to assemble the lasagna, carefully fish each strip out with your hands.

4. Preheat the oven to 350°F.

5. Assemble the lasagna in the baking dish. First spoon a cup of sauce in the bottom. Over that place a layer of lasagna noodles, overlapping the sides of the strips slightly. Spread a third of the ricotta cheese mixture over the noodles and cover it with another cup of sauce and then one quarter of the grated mozzarella. Add another layer of overlapping noodles strips, then another third of the ricotta cheese mixture, and cover with another cup of sauce and another quarter of the grated mozzarella; repeat that sequence one more time, ending with a fourth layer of lasagna. Top with the remaining sauce and mozzarella. Sprinkle with the Parmesan cheese, if desired.

6. Bake the lasagna, uncovered, for 45 to 60 minutes in the oven.

Vegetable Lasagna Roll-ups

This is a different version of lasagna, using vegetables instead of meat, in pretty, easy-to-make rolls.

Makes 12 roll-ups; serves 4 to 6

Ingredients

1 pound curly-edged lasagna
   noodles
1 tablespoon olive oil
10-ounce package frozen
   chopped spinach,
   defrosted
10-ounce package frozen
   broccoli florets, defrosted
2 cloves garlic
¼ cup fresh basil leaves or 1
   tablespoon dried basil
2 tablespoons parsley leaves,
   stems removed
2 cups (15-ounce container)
   ricotta cheese
1 egg
1 teaspoon salt
½ teaspoon freshly ground
   pepper
3 cups Tomato Sauce (page
   150)
¾ cup freshly grated
   Parmesan cheese

Equipment

Measuring cups
Measuring spoons
Large pot
Oven mitts
Paper towels
Small knife
Food processor
Large rectangular baking
   pan, about 9 × 13 × 3
   inches
Cutting board (optional)
Rubber spatula

1. In the large pot bring 8 quarts of water to a boil. Slowly add the lasagna noodles, a few at a time, and cook 8 to 10 minutes, or until they are tender but firm, *al dente*. You probably won't use all the lasagna noodles, but cook the whole amount because some strips will break, and some may stick to the bottom of the pot.

2. When the noodles are done, wear oven mitts and carry the pot to the sink. Add cold water to stop the cooking. As soon as the pot is cool enough to handle, pour out as much water as you can, still keeping the noodles in the pot. Add more cold water to cover the noodles and add the olive oil to prevent them from sticking together. When you're ready to assemble the lasagna, carefully fish each strip out with your hands.

3. While the noodles are cooking, squeeze all the water out of the chopped spinach with your hands and set it aside on a paper towel.

4. Separate the broccoli florets and pat them dry with a paper towel. Separate the heads into smaller florets and cut off any long stems, leaving about an inch on each floret. Set the florets aside and save the cut-off stems for another use.

5. Peel the garlic and process in a food processor with the basil and parsley. Add the ricotta cheese, egg, spinach, salt, and pepper, and process very briefly.

6. Preheat oven to 350°F.

7. Pour 1 cup of the Tomato Sauce in the bottom of the baking pan.

8. Lay one lasagna noodle flat on the counter or a cutting board, and spread ¼ cup of the ricotta-spinach mixture along the length

of the strip with a rubber spatula. Starting at one of the short ends, roll it up, making a plump roll-up. Tuck a broccoli floret stem-first into the center of each side — it will slide in easily — and leave the florets showing. Lay the lasagna roll-up seam side down over the sauce in the bottom of the baking pan. Assemble the rest of the roll-ups in the same manner, and lay them in the baking pan.

9. Pour the remaining sauce over the roll-ups, and sprinkle the Parmesan cheese over the top.

10. Bake for 25 to 30 minutes in the oven.

Steamed Rice

This is all-purpose rice, to use as a side dish, in soups, in salads, for rice pudding, and in other recipes.

Makes 3 cups

Ingredients
2 cups water
1 teaspoon salt
1 teaspoon butter (optional)
1 cup long-grain rice

Equipment
Measuring cups
Measuring spoons
Heavy 2-quart saucepan
   with lid
Fork

1. In the heavy saucepan bring the water, salt, and butter to a boil over high heat. Add the rice, lower the heat, and simmer, covered, for 20 minutes.

2. Remove the lid and put the fork gently through the rice to see if there is any water let in the bottom of the saucepan. If all the water is absorbed, fluff the rice with the fork; if not, cover and cook a minute or two longer.

Rice Pilaf

This is a tasty rice dish, popular in the Middle East. It lends itself to many variations.

Serves 4

Ingredients
2 tablespoons butter
1 small onion, peeled and
    finely chopped
1 cup long-grain rice
1½ cups chicken stock
Salt
Freshly ground pepper

Equipment
Measuring cups
Measuring spoons
Heavy 2-quart saucepan
    with lid
Wooden spoon

1. Melt the butter slowly over moderate heat in the saucepan. Add the chopped onion and sauté until soft, about 2 to 3 minutes, stirring occasionally with the wooden spoon. Add the rice and stir until the grains are well coated.

2. Add the chicken stock and bring to a boil. Cover the saucepan, reduce the heat to low, and simmer about 15 to 20 minutes, or until all the stock is absorbed.

3. Taste for seasoning and add salt and freshly ground pepper, if desired.

Variations

Nut and Currant Pilaf: Add ¼ cup currants with the chicken stock; stir in ¼ cup toasted, slivered almonds or toasted pine nuts at the end, after the rice is cooked.

Parsley Pilaf: Stir in 2 tablespoons finely chopped parsley at the end, after the rice is cooked.

Salads and Dressings

With the wide availability of fresh produce, the variety of greens and vegetables, and our interest in healthy eating, salads are now an important part of meal planning. You can serve them as a whole meal, a first course, the main dish, a zesty side dish to an entrée, or a palate cleanser after the main course. Wherever they appear, salads should be fresh, crisp, cool, and lightly dressed.

Salad Greens

These are some of the most popular varieties of greens.

Romaine has long, crisp, oval leaves in a large full head that is more tender toward the center.

Escarole, with large, broad, furled leaves that are sometimes tough on the outside, has a robust taste.

Boston Lettuce has soft, pale green leaves with a delicate flavor that grow in a loose head.

Bibb Lettuce is smaller than Boston, with a subtle flavor.

Red Leaf Lettuce has deep burgundy edges on soft ruffled leaves, and looks beautiful in a salad.

Green Leaf Lettuce has all-green, crinkly leaves and is similar to Red Leaf. Both grow loose-leaf and wilt quickly.

Salad Bowl is sweet and delicate, with long, thin leaves that look like elongated oak leaves. It's sold at farmers' markets.

Iceberg Lettuce has a tight head of bland, crisp leaves that shouldn't be separated before using and, except for the outer leaves, needn't be washed. It is available all year and keeps well.

Chicory has flat, spiky leaves of pale green and a slightly bitter taste, so it's used with milder greens.

Watercress has small, dark green leaves in bunches, and a peppery taste. It also goes well with citrus fruit salads.

Spinach can be used alone or with other greens. Use the young, small leaves, with stems removed.

Radicchio looks like small, gorgeous ruby-red cabbage with white veins. Its crisp, slightly bitter leaves add a stunning look and taste to a salad. It is expensive.

Arugula has narrow, flat, dark green leaves with a bitter peppery taste, and a small amount gives salad a punch.

Endive grows as a long, tight head of pale, crisp, slightly bitter leaves. It is very expensive.

Mixed Green Salad

A combination of greens makes a salad with interesting texture, taste, and color. Pick two or three varieties (see pages 168–169). In general, figure on two cups of greens and about 1 tablespoon of dressing per person.

Serves 4

Ingredients
8 cups (2 quarts) of fresh,
    crisp mixed greens

Equipment
Salad spinner
Paper towels
Salad bowl
Salad fork and spoon

1. The leaves of all greens except iceberg lettuce and endive need to be washed. Carefully separate the leaves and wash them under cold running water. Place them in the basket of a salad spinner and let them drain into the sink. Put the basket into the spinner and spin the leaves as dry as possible, emptying out the accumulated water once or twice.

2. Lay a strip of paper towels on the counter, and put a layer of clean greens on it. Cover them with another strip of towels, and repeat, until you have transferred all the greens. Cover with another strip of towels. Roll up the paper towels, and store in the crisper drawer of the refrigerator.

3. When you are ready to serve the salad, tear large leaves into smaller pieces and put in the salad bowl.

4. Mix the dressing of choice and pour it over the greens. With the salad fork and spoon gently toss the leaves over and over to coat them lightly.

 # Fresh Vegetable Salad

You can add several raw vegetables to a mixed green salad and turn it into a fairly substantial dish. Or garnish a salad course with one or two of the following.

Celery. Finely cut or dice the stalks, not the leaves.

Cucumber. Cut in thin slices, crosswise. Unless the skin is tough or has been waxed, you don't need to peel it. To crisp, soak the slices in salted ice water for 30 minutes.

Tomatoes. Slice large tomatoes, leave small cherry tomatoes whole.

Radishes. Slice them.

Avocado. Peel and slice just before using.

Carrots. Scrape, then shred or slice into thin slivers.

Scallions. Dice them.

Mushrooms. Wipe fresh mushrooms with a damp paper towel, then slice.

Green, red, and yellow peppers. Discard seeds and inner ribs, then cut into thin julienne slices.

Sprouts. Rinse and pat dry.

Summer Pasta Salad

Orzo is a small, rice-shaped pasta that makes a lovely salad.

Makes 4 cups; serves 6 to 8

Ingredients
1 cup orzo
¼ cup (½ recipe) Garlic
    Vinaigrette made with
    olive oil (page 190)
2 ounces feta or mozzarella
    cheese
8 cherry tomatoes
¼ cup chopped pitted black
    olives
¼ cup chopped parsley
¼ cup minced basil
Salt
Freshly ground pepper

Equipment
Measuring cups
Large mixing bowl
Cutting board
Knife
Mixing spoon

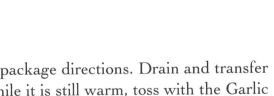

1. Cook orzo according to package directions. Drain and transfer to a large mixing bowl. While it is still warm, toss with the Garlic Vinaigrette. Set aside to cool.

2. Cut the cheese into small dice, about ¼-inch cubes.

3. Cut small cherry tomatoes in half and large ones in quarters.

173

4. Add the cheese, tomatoes, black olives, parsley, and basil to the orzo and toss to combine well. Taste for seasoning and add salt and freshly ground pepper as needed.

5. Serve at room temperature. If you aren't going to serve the salad promply, cover it with plastic wrap and refrigerate it. Let it return to room temperature before you serve it.

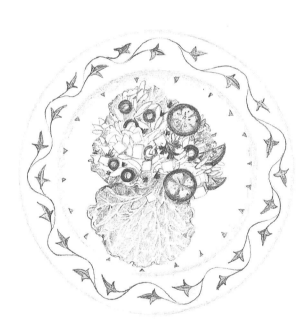

Winter Pasta Salad

This salad combines pasta with ratatouille. You can use leftover ratatouille — the proportions of each really don't matter.

Makes 7 cups; serves 8 to 10

Ingredients
8 ounces rotelle
2 to 3 tablespoons olive oil
4 cups (⅓ recipe) Ratatouille
    (page 136)
Salt
Freshly ground pepper
2 tablespoons chopped fresh
    basil or parsley

Equipment
Measuring cups
Measuring spoons
Colander
Large mixing bowl
Mixing spoons

1. Cook pasta according to package directions. Drain in a colander and transfer to a large mixing bowl. While the pasta is still warm, toss with enough olive oil to moisten it. Set aside to cool.

2. Add the Ratatouille and combine well. Taste for seasoning and add salt and freshly ground pepper as needed.

3. Sprinkle the top with the fresh basil or parsley and serve at room temperature. If you aren't going to serve the salad promptly, cover it with plastic wrap and refrigerate it. Let it return to room temperature and garnish it with the fresh herbs just before serving.

Rice Salad

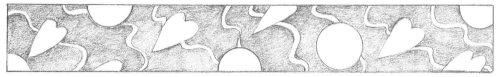

This rice dish features traditional salad vegetables, but you could add practically any other vegetable or cooked meat cut bite-sized.

Makes 6 cups; serves 6 to 8

Ingredients

1 cup raw rice
2 to 3 tablespoons vegetable
  oil
3 scallions
1 medium cucumber
1 small red pepper
2 medium tomatoes
2 tablespoons chopped basil
2 tablespoons chopped
  parsley
¼ cup (½ recipe) Vinaigrette
  (page 189)
Salt
Freshly ground pepper

Equipment

Measuring cups
Measuring spoons
Heavy 2-quart saucepan
Large mixing bowl
Mixing spoon
Mixing fork
Cutting board
Knife
Vegetable peeler
Large serving or salad bowl

1. Cook rice according to Steamed Rice, page 165. Transfer to a large mixing bowl, and while it is still warm, add the vegetable oil 1 tablespoon at a time, tossing after each addition with the large mixing spoon and fork until all the rice is moistened. Set aside to cool.

2. Clean the scallions, slice them finely, and put them in a large serving or salad bowl. Peel, seed, and dice the cucumber and add to the bowl. Core and seed the red pepper and cut into small pieces. Cut the tomatoes in half, squeeze out as much juice as you can, seed them, and cut into small pieces. As you prepare each vegetable, put it in the large serving or salad bowl.

3. Add the chopped basil, the parsley, and the cooled rice to the vegetables and combine well. Using the large fork and spoon, toss the mixture with the Vinaigrette. Taste for seasoning and add salt and freshly ground pepper as needed.

4. Serve at room temperature. If you aren't going to serve the salad promptly, cover it with plastic wrap and refrigerate it. Let it return to room temperature before serving.

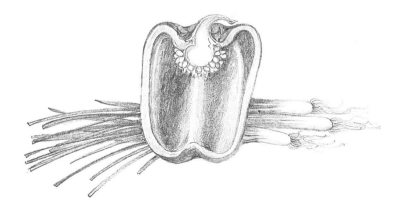

Brown Rice Salad

Serve this rice salad with chicken or meat dishes, especially curries.

Makes about 6 cups; serves 6 to 8

Ingredients
1 cup raw brown rice
¼ cup (½ recipe) French
    Dressing made with
    vegetable oil and a fruit
    vinegar (page 189)
½ cup (2-ounce package)
    slivered almonds
½ cup dried currants
¼ cup chopped parsley
Salt
Freshly ground pepper

Equipment
Measuring cups
Large serving or salad bowl
Mixing spoon
Mixing fork
Baking pan
Oven mitts

1. Position an oven rack at least 4 inches from the source of heat and preheat the broiler.

2. Cook the brown rice according to package directions. Transfer to the large serving or salad bowl, and while it is still warm, toss with the French Dressing, using the mixing fork and spoon. Set aside to cool.

3. Scatter the almonds in the bottom of the baking pan in one layer. Put the pan under the broiler for several minutes to brown the almonds lightly, taking care that the almonds don't burn.

4. Add the lightly toasted almonds, currants, and parsley to the rice and toss to combine well. Taste for seasoning and add salt and freshly ground pepper as needed.

5. Serve at room temperature. If you aren't going to serve the salad promptly, cover it with plastic wrap and refrigerate it. Let it return to room temperature before serving.

Bulgur Wheat Salad

This fresh, lemony, minty-tasting cracked wheat salad comes from the Middle East, where it is called *tabbouleh*. Serve it in a bowl lined with leaves of romaine lettuce.

Makes 4 cups, serves 6 to 8

Ingredients
1 cup bulgur
2 medium ripe tomatoes
2 scallions
¼ cup chopped mint leaves
¾ cup chopped parsley
⅓ cup olive oil
¼ cup (about 1 lemon) fresh
    lemon juice
Salt
Freshly ground pepper

Equipment
Measuring cups
Medium mixing bowl
Cutting board
Knife
Serving or salad bowl
Colander

1. Put the bulgur in the mixing bowl and cover with 1 cup cold water. Let stand for 30 minutes.

2. Meanwhile, cut the tomatoes in half, squeeze to remove juice, remove the seeds and core, and cut them into small pieces. Put them in the serving or salad bowl.

3. Slice the scallions thinly and add them to the tomatoes.

4. If any liquid is left in the bulgur, drain it through the colander. Add the bulgur to the tomatoes and scallions in the serving bowl and stir in the chopped mint and parsley.

5. Pour the olive oil and lemon juice over, and toss well. Taste for seasoning, and add salt and freshly ground pepper as needed.

Note: Bulgur is available by itself and also packaged with the appropriate dried spices. If you use the packaged tabbouleh mix, use half the amount of fresh mint leaves and parsley.

Chef's Salad

This is a traditional recipe for chef's salad. You can substitute turkey for chicken and tongue for ham and, in fact, use other favorite cold meats and cheeses.

Serves 4

Ingredients
1 head romaine lettuce
1½ cups cooked chicken
1½ cups cooked ham
4 ounces Swiss cheese
1 recipe French Dressing
    (page 189) or Herb
    Vinaigrette (page 190)
Salt
Freshly ground pepper
¼ cup crumbled blue cheese
2 large tomatoes, quartered,
    or 8 cherry tomatoes
4 hard-boiled eggs, halved

Equipment
Measuring cups
Cutting board
Knife
Salad spinner
Salad or serving bowl
Salad servers

1. Wash and dry the lettuce leaves and refrigerate until ready to assemble the salad.

2. Cut the chicken, ham, and Swiss cheese into thin matchstick strips, and put them in the salad or serving bowl. Moisten with

half the dressing and toss well with the salad servers. Taste for seasoning and add salt and freshly ground pepper, as needed.

3. Tear up the lettuce leaves and add to the bowl. Add the remaining dressing and toss gently to moisten the lettuce. Sprinkle the salad with crumbled blue cheese, and garnish with the tomatoes and hard-boiled eggs.

Tuna Salad Niçoise

This is a traditional dish in southern France. Serve it with crusty French bread, and you have lunch or a hot-weather dinner.

Serves 6

Ingredients

1 cup fresh or 1 (9-ounce) package frozen green beans

12 small or 6 large new potatoes

1 head Boston or Bibb lettuce

1 recipe Mustard Vinaigrette (page 190)

1 tablespoon finely cut dill

2 (6½-ounce) cans tuna fish

1 tablespoon chopped scallions

½ cup halved, pitted black olives

3 large tomatoes, quartered, or 12 cherry tomatoes

6 hard-boiled eggs, halved

Equipment

Measuring cups

Measuring spoons

Salad spinner

Small mixing bowl

Salad bowl

Fork

Salad servers

1. Cook the green beans just until crisp-tender (see page 127) and refrigerate if not using right away.

2. Cook the new potatoes (see page 140) and refrigerate if not using right away. Cut large ones in half.

3. Wash and dry the lettuce leaves.

4. In a small bowl mix the Mustard Vinaigrette and dill.

5. Drain the tuna fish and put into the large salad bowl. Flake the tuna fish with the fork and moisten with half the dressing.

6. Add the green beans, new potatoes, scallions, and black olives, and mix lightly with salad servers.

7. Tear up the lettuce leaves and add to the bowl. Add the remaining dressing and toss gently to coat all the lettuce. Garnish the salad with the tomatoes and hard-boiled eggs.

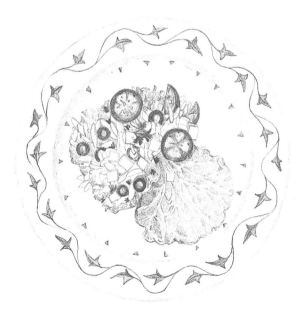

Chicken Salad

Serves 4

Ingredients

1 head Bibb or romaine
    lettuce
1 small red pepper
1 stalk celery without the
    leafy top
4 cups cooked bite-sized
    chicken pieces
2 tablespoons thinly sliced
    scallions
½ cup walnut pieces or
    salted cashews
1 cup Sour Cream Dressing
    (page 194)
Salt
Freshly ground pepper

Equipment

Measuring cups
Measuring spoons
Cutting board
Knife
Large mixing bowl
2 large spoons

1. Wash and dry the lettuce.

2. Quarter and seed the red pepper, cut it into thin strips, and put them in the mixing bowl.

3. Cut the celery stalk into thin slices and add to the bowl.

186

4. Add the chicken, scallions, and nuts to the bowl. Add the Sour Cream Dressing and toss until well mixed. Taste for seasoning and mix in salt and pepper, as needed.

5. Mound on a bed of lettuce on a large platter or on individual plates.

Salad Dressings

Delicately flavored lettuces such as Bibb, Boston, green and red leaf, and salad bowl go best with a dressing made with a light, delicate olive or vegetable oil; robustly flavored greens such as romaine, escarole, chicory, iceberg, and spinach can take a dressing made with a more strongly flavored oil. Taste different oils to find the ones you like best. Also experiment with different vinegars — red or white wine vinegar, balsamic vinegar — to see which you like with which oil.

French or Vinaigrette Dressing

This is a basic vinaigrette dressing to which you can add other flavors, such as garlic, herbs, mustard.

Makes more than ½ cup

Ingredients
2 tablespoons vinegar (or
    part lemon juice)
½ teaspoon salt
Several grindings of fresh
    pepper
½ cup olive or vegetable oil

Equipment
Measuring cups
Measuring spoons
Small mixing bowl
Wire whisk

1. In the small mixing bowl combine the vinegar and salt. Stir in several grindings of fresh pepper.

2. Gradually add the oil, beating it in with the wire whisk.

3. Taste the dressing to adjust the seasonings. You may want to add a little more salt or pepper or vinegar.

4. If you aren't using the dressing at once, store it in a tightly capped jar and shake well before using.

Variations

Garlic Vinaigrette: Put a peeled split clove of garlic in the bottle to season the dressing.

Herb Vinaigrette: Stir in 1 tablespoon of finely snipped fresh tarragon or basil.

Mustard Vinaigrette: Stir in 1 teaspoon dry mustard before adding the oil.

Mayonnaise

Store-bought mayonnaise is a great convenience, and you can give it a homemade taste by adding other flavorings. For pure mayonnaise taste, nothing beats homemade, but that requires raw eggs, which should not be eaten. Raw eggs sometimes carry salmonella bacteria, which are eliminated by cooking.

Tangy Mayonnaise: To 1 cup of mayonnaise stir in 1 teaspoon fresh lemon juice or Worcestershire sauce.

Dill Mayonnaise: To 1 cup of mayonnaise stir in 1 teaspoon dry mustard and 1 tablespoon finely minced fresh dill sprigs.

Russian Dressing

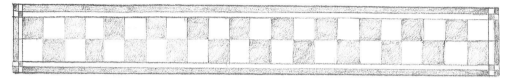

Makes 1½ cups

Ingredients
1 cup mayonnaise
½ cup chili sauce
2 tablespoons minced green
    pepper
2 tablespoons finely cut
    celery
Salt
Freshly ground pepper

Equipment
Medium mixing bowl
Measuring cups
Measuring spoons
Mixing spoon

1. In the mixing bowl combine the mayonnaise, chili sauce, green pepper, and celery. Taste for seasoning and add salt and freshly ground pepper as needed. Refrigerate until ready to use.

Yogurt Dressing

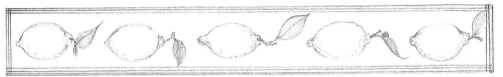

This is good over vegetable salad.

Makes about 1 cup

Ingredients
1 cup plain yogurt
2 tablespoons fresh lemon
    juice (about half a
    lemon)
Salt
Freshly ground pepper

Equipment
Measuring cup
Measuring spoons
Small mixing bowl
Mixing spoon

1. In the small mixing bowl combine the yogurt and lemon juice. Taste for seasoning and add salt and freshly ground pepper as needed. Refrigerate until ready to use.

Variation

Herbed Yogurt Dressing: Add any or all of these — dill, chives, parsley, tarragon — using a total of about 2 tablespoons finely minced herbs.

Sour Cream Dressing

This is good with fruit, vegetable, and chicken salads.

Makes about 1 cup

Ingredients
1 cup sour cream
2 tablespoons fresh lemon
    juice (about half a
    lemon)
Salt
Freshly ground pepper

Equipment
Measuring cup
Measuring spoons
Small mixing bowl
Mixing spoon

1. In the small mixing bowl combine the sour cream and lemon juice. Taste for seasoning and add salt and freshly ground pepper as needed. Refrigerate until ready to use.

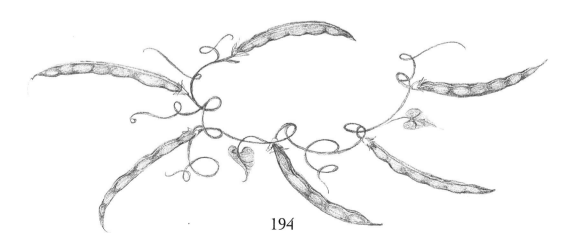

Honey Poppy-Seed Dressing

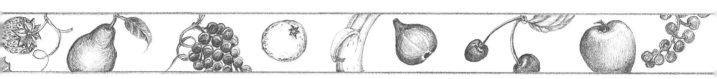

This is lovely on fruit salads.

Makes about 1 cup

Ingredients
1 cup plain yogurt
1 tablespoon raspberry
    vinegar
2 tablespoons honey
1 tablespoon poppy seeds
Salt
Freshly ground pepper

Equipment
Measuring cup
Measuring spoons
Small mixing bowl
Mixing spoon

1. In the small mixing bowl combine the yogurt, vinegar, honey, and poppy seeds. Taste for seasoning and add salt and freshly ground pepper as needed. Refrigerate until ready to use.

195

Cakes and Pies

Chocolate Cake

Makes one 8-inch-square cake

Ingredients

For preparing the pan:
1 to 2 teaspoons butter, at
    room temperature
1 to 2 tablespoons flour
For the cake:
2 ounces (squares)
    unsweetened chocolate
8 tablespoons (1 stick)
    butter at room
    temperature
1 cup sugar
2 eggs
1 teaspoon vanilla
1 cup flour
½ teaspoon cream of tartar
½ teaspoon baking soda
½ teaspoon salt
½ cup milk
¼ cup confectioners' sugar

Equipment

8-inch-square baking pan
Measuring cups
Measuring spoons
Double boiler
Wooden spoon
Electric mixer
Sifter
Mixing bowls
Cake tester
Oven mitts
Cake rack

1. Preheat the oven to 350°F. Butter and flour the baking pan.

2. In the double boiler melt the chocolate over hot but not boiling water, stirring occasionally with the wooden spoon. Remove from the heat and let cool.

3. With the electric mixer cream the butter and slowly add the sugar, beating until light and fluffy. Beat in the eggs, one at a time. Stir in the vanilla and the cooled chocolate.

4. Sift together the flour, cream of tartar, baking soda, and salt into another bowl.

5. With the mixer at moderate speed, gradually add half the flour mixture to the chocolate mixture, then add the milk, still beating, and the remaining flour mixture.

6. Spoon the batter into the prepared pan, and bake 25 to 30 minutes, or until the cake tester inserted in the middle comes out clean.

7. Remove cake from the oven, wearing oven mitts, and let it cool in the pan for 10 minutes. Then turn it out on the cake rack and turn it right side up.

8. When the cake is cool, sift the confectioners' sugar over it.

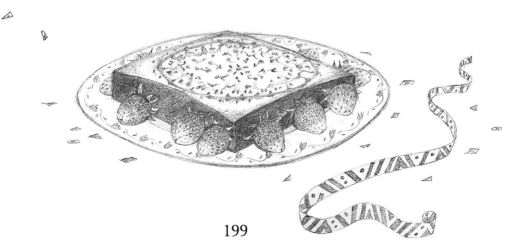

Sponge Cake

Makes two 8-inch-round layers

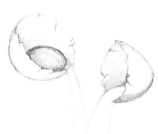

Ingredients

1 cup flour
1¼ teaspoons baking powder
¼ teaspoon salt
4 eggs
1 tablespoon fresh lemon
    juice
1½ tablespoons cold water
1 teaspoon vanilla
1 cup sugar
Quick Caramel Frosting
    (page 214)

Equipment

Two 8-inch-round cake pans
Waxed paper
Scissors
Measuring cups
Measuring spoons
Sifter
Small mixing bowl
Electric mixer with 2 bowls
Rubber spatula
Cake tester
Oven mitts
Cake racks
Narrow flat spatula

1. Preheat the oven to 325°F. Cut two 8-inch circles out of waxed paper and set them in the bottoms of two 8-inch-round cake pans.

2. Sift together the flour, baking powder, and salt into the small bowl and set aside.

3. Separate the eggs (see page 20). Put the whites in one bowl

200

of the electric mixer and set aside. Put the yolks in the second bowl of the electric mixer.

4. Beat the egg yolks with the lemon juice, water, and vanilla until thick. Gradually beat in ¾ cup of the sugar. Set the mixing bowl aside.

5. With the electric mixer and clean, dry beaters beat the egg whites until they stand in soft peaks, then gradually beat in the remaining ¼ cup sugar, beating until the egg whites are stiff but not dry.

6. With the rubber spatula gently fold the beaten egg whites into the yolk mixture a few times, then sprinkle the sifted flour mixture over the eggs and fold it in gently until no dry flour shows. Be careful not to blend too vigorously or you will lose the air bubbles that make the cake light.

7. Spoon the batter into the prepared pans and set them on a center shelf in the oven. Bake about 25 to 30 minutes, or until the cake shrinks from the edges of the pan and the cake tester inserted in the center comes out clean.

8. Wearing oven mitts, remove each pan from the oven and turn them upside down on the cake racks to cool. When the pans are cold, remove the layers, using the spatula if necessary. Peel off the waxed paper rounds from the bottoms of the layers.

9. After the layers have cooled, place one layer on a plate. With the narrow flat spatula spread the layer with ¼ of the frosting. Set the other layer over it and cover it with ⅓ of the remaining frosting. Use the rest of the frosting for the sides of the cake.

Ice Cream Cake

Makes a double-layer 8-inch-round cake

Ingredients
Sponge Cake (page 200)
1 quart of your favorite ice
    cream, slightly softened

Equipment
Aluminum foil
Rubber spatula

1. Lay one layer of the cake on a large sheet of aluminum foil. Spread the softened ice cream over the layer, using the rubber spatula.

2. Place the second layer on top and carefully bring the sides of the aluminum foil up over the cake to enclose it. Store in the freezer until you are ready to serve it.

Carrot Cake

This is rich with nuts and raisins and is baked in an angel cake pan for a festive appearance.

Makes one 10-inch cake; serves 10 to 12

Ingredients

For preparing the pan:
1 tablespoon butter
4 tablespoons flour

For the cake:
4 medium carrots (about 2 cups grated)
½ pound (2 sticks) butter, softened
1 cup granulated sugar
1 cup light brown sugar
4 eggs
3 cups flour
2 teaspoons baking powder
1 teaspoon baking soda
1 teaspoon salt
2 teaspoons ground cinnamon
½ teaspoon ground nutmeg
2 tablespoons fresh lemon juice
2 tablespoons orange juice
1 cup chopped walnuts or pecans
1 cup raisins
1 tablespoon confectioners' sugar

Equipment

10-inch angel cake pan with removable bottom
Measuring cups
Measuring spoons
Vegetable peeler
Grater or food processor
Waxed paper
Electric mixer
Sifter
Large bowl
Medium bowl
Rubber spatula
Oven mitts
Cake tester
Knife or narrow metal spatula
Cake rack
Small sieve

203

1. Preheat the oven to 350°F. Butter and flour the angel cake pan, including the tube.

2. Scrape the carrots with the vegetable peeler. Using the medium side of the grater set on a piece of waxed paper, or the grater blade of the food processor, grate the carrots and set them aside.

3. Using the electric mixer, cream the butter in the large bowl until light and fluffy. Gradually beat in the granulated sugar. Gradually add the brown sugar, pressing out any lumps, and beat well after each addition. Beat another 2 minutes.

4. Add the eggs, one at a time, and beat well after each addition.

5. Sift together the flour, baking powder, baking soda, salt, cinnamon, and nutmeg into the medium bowl.

6. With the electric mixer at low speed, slowly beat 1 cup of the flour mixture into the creamed butter and sugar, then add the lemon juice. Slowly beat in another cup of the flour mixture, then the orange juice, and finally add the rest of the flour mixture, beating just until smooth.

7. With a rubber spatula, stir in the grated carrots, nuts, and raisins.

8. Spoon the batter into the prepared tube pan, distributing it evenly around the pan, and bake 50 to 60 minutes, or until the cake tester inserted in the center of the cake comes out clean.

9. Wearing oven mitts, remove the cake from the oven. Let it cool in the pan about 15 minutes. Carefully loosen the cake by running the knife or narrow spatula around the inside edges. Remove the outer rim and put the cake (still on the bottom of the cake tin) on a wire rack and let it cool completely.

10. When the cake is completely cool, in about an hour, loosen it from the bottom and sides of the cake-tin tube, remove, and sift confectioners' sugar over the top through the small sieve.

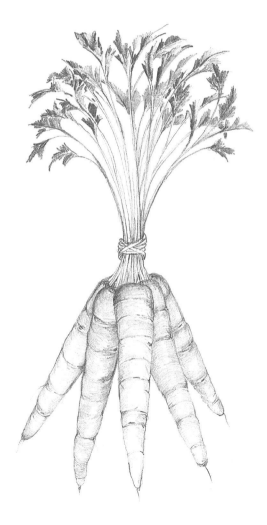

Gingerbread

Makes one 9-inch-square cake

Ingredients

For preparing the pan:
1 to 2 teaspoons butter
1 tablespoon flour

For the gingerbread:
8 tablespoons (1 stick)
    butter
1 cup molasses
2½ cups flour
½ teaspoon salt
1½ teaspoons baking soda
1 teaspoon ground ginger
½ teaspoon ground
    cinnamon
¼ teaspoon ground cloves
¼ teaspoon ground nutmeg
1 cup sour cream
1 teaspoon vanilla

Equipment

9-inch-square cake pan
Measuring cups
Measuring spoons
Heavy saucepan
Sifter
Large mixing bowl
Mixing spoon
Oven mitts
Cake tester

1. Preheat the oven to 350°F. Butter and flour the cake pan.

2. In the heavy saucepan melt the butter and stir in the molasses. Remove from the heat.

3. Sift the flour, salt, baking soda, ginger, cinnamon, cloves, and nutmeg into the large mixing bowl. Stir in the butter and molasses mixture. Add the sour cream and vanilla and stir well.

4. Spoon the batter into the baking pan, and bake about 25 to 30 minutes, or until the cake tester comes out clean, the top is dry, and the gingerbread shrinks from the sides of the pan.

5. Wearing oven mitts, remove the gingerbread from the oven.

6. Cut into squares and serve warm, topped with Whipped Cream (page 262) or warm applesauce.

Apple Cobbler

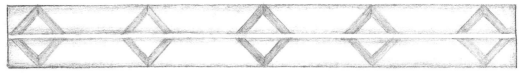

This is sometimes called a crunch or a crisp, but whatever name you give it, it's warm spicy apples under a crisp crumbled topping. Serve it warm with cream or whipped cream.

Serves 6

Ingredients

For preparing the casserole:
1 tablespoon butter
For the cobbler:
1½ pounds tart firm apples,
    such as Granny Smiths
¼ cup water
¾ cup flour
1 cup light brown sugar
1 teaspoon cinnamon
8 tablespoons (1 stick)
    butter

Equipment

1½-quart casserole
Measuring cups
Measuring spoons
Knife
Mixing bowl
Pastry blender
Oven mitts
Fork or cake tester

1. Preheat the oven to 350°F. and butter the casserole.

2. Quarter, peel, and core the apples, then slice them about ½ inch thick. Scatter them in the bottom of the prepared casserole. Unless the apples are very juicy, pour the water over them.

3. In the mixing bowl combine the flour, brown sugar, and cin-

208

namon. Cut the butter into 8 pieces and blend it into the mixture with the pastry blender until it looks like oatmeal. Spread it evenly over the apples.

4. Bake about 30 minutes, or until the crust is brown and the apples are tender when tested with the fork or cake tester.

5. Wearing the oven mitts, remove the cobbler from the oven.

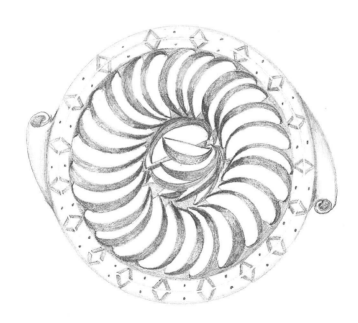

Old-Fashioned Strawberry Shortcake

Strawberries are traditional, but there's no reason you can't use raspberries, peaches, or any favorite fruit, sliced and sugared.

Makes 8 shortcakes

Ingredients

For the biscuits:
2 cups flour
4 teaspoons baking powder
1 teaspoon salt
1 tablespoon sugar
Dash nutmeg
8 tablespoons (1 stick)
    butter
½ cup milk plus up to 4
    tablespoons more
For the filling and garnish:
1 quart berries
Superfine sugar to taste
1 cup (half pint) heavy
    cream
2 tablespoons butter,
    softened

Equipment

Measuring cups
Measuring spoons
Sifter
Large mixing bowl
Pastry blender
Fork
Nonstick cookie sheet
Metal mixing bowl for
    whipping the cream
Rotary hand beater
Mixing bowl for strawberries
Knife
Plastic wrap
Oven mitts
Serving platter
Spoon

1. Preheat the oven to 425°F.

2. Sift the flour, baking powder, salt, sugar, and nutmeg into the mixing bowl. Add the butter, a tablespoon at a time, and cut it into the flour with the pastry blender until it looks like cornmeal.

3. Add ½ cup of the milk a little at a time, mixing with a fork until the dough is soft but not sticky, then add a tablespoon at a time until it forms a ball. You may not need all the milk.

4. Divide the dough into 8 pieces. With your hands shape each piece into a small ball about 2 inches in diameter. Flatten it with the palm of your hand until it is about ½ inch thick.

5. Place the rounds of dough about an inch apart on the ungreased cookie sheet and bake about 12 to 15 minutes, or until the biscuits are golden.

6. Meanwhile, chill the metal mixing bowl and the rotary beater in the refrigerator.

7. Slice the strawberries into another mixing bowl, setting aside 8 of the best-looking whole ones to decorate each shortcake. Sweeten to taste with a little sugar.

8. Beat the cream in the chilled bowl just until it stands up in peaks when you lift the beaters. Cover the bowl with plastic wrap and refrigerate.

9. When the biscuits are done, remove them from the oven (wearing the oven mitts), split them in half, and put them on a serving platter. Lightly butter each bottom half, spoon on some of the sliced, sweetened berries, and cover with the top half of the biscuit. Spoon a dollop of whipped cream over the top, and decorate with a strawberry. Serve at once while the biscuits are still warm.

Frostings

Here are some guidelines for easy frosting:

◆ If you are going to frost the sides as well as the top of a cake, lay four pieces of waxed paper on an extra-large plate so that each piece covers one quarter of the plate and extends beyond the rim. That way you can pull each piece of paper out later without disturbing the frosted cake.

◆ Set the cake on the plate over the pieces of waxed paper. Spread the frosting around the sides first, then pile all the rest on the top and swirl it around with a spatula. Don't try to make a smooth surface; a slightly uneven look is more appealing.

◆ If you are frosting a layer cake, put the bottom layer upside down on the waxed paper so that the flat side is up. Spread the filling on it, then put the top layer over it, flat side down. Frost the sides and then the top, as above.

◆ The first time you make cooked frosting, you may find it is a little too thick or too thin. If it is sugary, add a little lemon juice. If it is runny, add a little sifted confectioners' sugar until it's the right consistency to spread. If it's too thick, whisk in a little hot water or milk to thin it.

◆ The easiest way to fill a layer cake is with jam or sliced and sweetened fruit in place of frosting, and the easiest way to frost the top of a cake is with a dusting of sifted confectioners' sugar.

Portsmouth Frosting

Makes about 1½ cups

Ingredients
¼ cup cream
1 teaspoon vanilla
2 tablespoons butter, melted
2½ to 3 cups confectioners'
    sugar

Equipment
Measuring cups
Measuring spoons
Large mixing bowl
Wooden spoon
Sifter
Small bowl

1. In the large mixing bowl combine the cream, vanilla, and melted butter and stir with the wooden spoon.

2. Sift the confectioners' sugar into the small bowl and with the wooden spoon beat it into the creamy mixture, a little at a time, until it is thick enough to spread. You may not need all the sugar.

Quick Caramel Frosting

Makes 1½ cups

Ingredients
8 tablespoons (1 stick)
    butter
½ cup dark brown sugar
¼ cup milk
1¾ to 2 cups confectioners'
    sugar
1 teaspoon vanilla

Equipment
Measuring cups
Measuring spoons
Heavy saucepan
Wooden spoon
Electric mixer

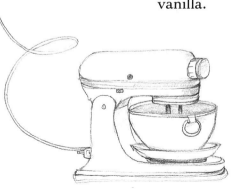

1. In the heavy saucepan melt the butter over low heat. Add the brown sugar and stir until the sugar melts. Stir in the milk. Remove the pan from the heat and let cool.

2. With the electric mixer beat in the confectioners' sugar, a little at a time, until the frosting is thick enough to spread. Stir in the vanilla.

Chocolate Fudge Frosting

Makes about 2 cups

Ingredients

1¾ cups sugar
⅛ teaspoon salt
2 ounces (squares)
    unsweetened chocolate,
    cut into bits
⅔ cup milk or light cream
2 tablespoons butter
2 tablespoons light corn
    syrup
1 teaspoon vanilla

Equipment

Measuring cups
Measuring spoons
Heavy saucepan
Wooden spoon
Electric hand mixer

1. In the heavy saucepan combine the sugar, salt, chocolate bits, milk or cream, butter, and corn syrup. Bring to a boil over moderate heat, and cook for 2 to 3 minutes, stirring constantly with the wooden spoon.

2. Remove from the heat and let cool slightly. Stir in the vanilla and beat with an electric hand mixer for about 5 to 7 minutes, or until the frosting is thick enough to spread.

Quick Chocolate Frosting

Makes about 1⅓ cups

Ingredients
8 ounces (squares)
    semisweet chocolate
8 tablespoons (1 stick)
    butter
1 teaspoon vanilla

Equipment
Measuring spoons
Double boiler
Electric hand mixer

1. Melt the chocolate and butter in the top of the double boiler over hot but not boiling water. Remove the top of the boiler from the heat and let the chocolate mixture cool slightly.

2. Stir in the vanilla and, using the electric hand mixer, beat the frosting until it is thick enough to spread. Don't worry if it looks runny; it solidifies as it cools.

Graham Cracker Crust

This is as easy — and good — as a pie shell gets. If you prefer, you can substitute gingersnaps, zwieback, vanilla or chocolate wafers for the graham crackers. Fill it with the Lemon Pie recipe that follows, or with a pudding or ice cream.

Makes one 9-inch pie shell

Ingredients
6 tablespoons (¾ stick)
    butter
1½ cups fine graham cracker
    crumbs
¼ cup confectioners' sugar

Equipment
Measuring cups
Heavy saucepan
Food processor, optional
Mixing bowl
Mixing spoon
9-inch glass pie pan
Fork
Oven mitts

1. Preheat the oven to 325°F.

2. In the heavy saucepan melt the butter, then let it cool.

3. If you don't have packaged graham cracker crumbs, spin whole crackers in the food processor until you have processed 1½ cups.

4. Put the graham cracker crumbs into the mixing bowl and stir

in the confectioners' sugar, combining them well. Stir in the melted butter and mix thoroughly with a fork.

5. Spoon the mixture into the pie pan and, using your fingers, press it as evenly as possible over the bottom and around the sides of the pan.

6. Bake the shell for about 8 to 10 minutes, remove from the oven, wearing the mitts, and let it cool.

You can also use an unbaked shell for fillings that don't have too much liquid, such as puddings, if you chill it for at least two hours, until the crust is absolutely firm.

Lemon Pie

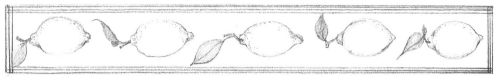

This is a great make-ahead dessert.

Serves 6 to 8

Ingredients

8 tablespoons (1 stick)
    butter
3 lemons
6 eggs
1¾ cups superfine sugar
1 cup heavy cream
1 Graham Cracker Crust
    (page 217), prebaked
12 to 16 fresh whole
    strawberries (optional)

Equipment

Measuring cups
Double boiler
Grater
Waxed paper
Knife
Hand juicer
Small sieve
Glass measuring cup
2 medium bowls
Wire whisk
Wooden spoon
Plastic wrap
Small metal mixing bowl
Rotary hand beater
Rubber spatula

1. In the top of the double boiler melt the butter over hot but not boiling water. Remove the top portion of the double boiler and let the butter cool.

2. Place the grater on a sheet of waxed paper and grate the rinds

of the three lemons, using the finest side of the grater. Grate only the yellow rind, not the white skin underneath. Set the waxed paper with the grated rind aside.

3. Cut the rindless lemons in half and juice them in the hand juicer. As the juicer fills up, empty it into the glass measuring cup. If the juicer doesn't have a built-in strainer to catch the pulp and the pits, pour the juice through the sieve into the measuring cup.

4. In one of the medium bowls beat the eggs well with the wire whisk. Add the sugar gradually, beating continuously. Stir in the lemon juice and rind.

5. Pour the mixture into the cooled butter and replace the top of the double boiler over the bottom. Cook the mixture over hot but not boiling water, stirring constantly with the wooden spoon until the filling is thick.

6. Pour the lemon filling into the other medium bowl, cover with plastic wrap, and chill in the refrigerator.

7. A half hour before you are ready to assemble the pie, put the small metal bowl and the rotary hand beater in the refrigerator to chill. Then whip the cream in the chilled bowl until it holds its shape in soft peaks.

8. Pour the lemon filling into the prepared Graham Cracker Crust, scraping it out of the bowl with the rubber spatula, and spread the whipped cream over the top. Decorate with fresh strawberries, if desired.

Single-Crust Pie Pastry

This is a good all-purpose recipe for a single prebaked pie crust, also called a pie shell. You can use this same recipe for an unbaked pie shell that is filled and then baked.

Makes one 9-inch pie shell

Ingredients

1½ cups flour plus 3 to 4 tablespoons for rolling out the dough
½ teaspoon salt
½ cup chilled vegetable shortening
3 to 4 tablespoons ice-cold water

Equipment

Measuring cups
Measuring spoons
Sifter
Large mixing bowl
Pastry blender
Fork
Pastry board
Rolling pin
9-inch metal pie plate
Scissors
Waxed paper
Oven mitts

1. Preheat the oven to 425°F.

2. Sift the 1½ cups of flour and the salt into the large mixing bowl and add the chilled vegetable shortening.

221

3. Using the pastry blender, cut the shortening into the flour until it looks like grains of rice.

4. Pour 3 tablespoons of the ice water over the dough and toss it lightly with the fork until blended and you can shape it into a compact ball. If it is still crumbly, mix in the remaining tablespoon of ice water and form into a ball.

5. Lay a pastry board on the counter and dust it with a little extra flour. Set the ball of dough in the center of the floured board, sprinkle a little flour on it, and pat it into a 4-inch circle.

6. Place the rolling pin across the middle of the dough and roll it out in continuous strokes, lifting the rolling pin as you get to the edge. Work your way around the dough in the same way, always starting with the rolling pin across the middle and raising it near the edge. If the dough gets a little sticky, sprinkle a little flour on it. When you have rolled the dough out in every direction, you should have a rough circle about 14 inches in diameter. If it is appreciably smaller, repeat the rolling process with a light touch.

7. To transfer the dough to the pie plate, lay the rolling pin across the center of the finished circle, and fold the bottom half of dough up and over the rolling pin. Hold the rolling pin with the draped dough over the pie plate, and unroll the dough into it, gently fitting it into the bottom and up the sides without stretching it. Leaving about a 1-inch rim of dough hanging over the edge of the pie plate, cut off the excess with the scissors; wrap it in waxed paper and refrigerate it, in case you need it to patch any tears in the dough.

8. Fold the overhanging dough under, making a double thickness around the edge of the plate, and crimp it by pressing the fork lightly into the doubled dough all around the rim.

9. Prick the bottom of the dough all over with the fork, place the pie plate on the bottom shelf of the oven, and bake for 12 to 15 minutes, or until the crust is lightly browned. Check the crust after 5 minutes, and if any spots have bubbled up, push them down with the back of a spoon. With oven mitts on, remove the crust from the oven. Let it cool before filling it.

Pecan Pie

This is rich and very nutty. It's traditionally served with unsweetened whipped cream.

Makes one 9-inch pie

Ingredients
2 tablespoons butter
3 eggs
½ cup dark brown sugar
1 cup dark corn syrup
1 teaspoon vanilla
1 tablespoon flour
1½ cups pecan halves or
    large pieces
One Single-Crust Pie Pastry,
    unbaked (page 221)
Whipped Cream (page 262),
    optional

Equipment
Measuring cups
Measuring spoons
Small saucepan
Electric mixer
Wooden spoon
Cookie sheet
Oven mitts

1. Preheat the oven to 350°F.

2. In the small saucepan melt the butter, remove from the heat, and let it cool.

3. Using the electric mixer, beat the eggs until light and fluffy.

224

Still beating, add the sugar, corn syrup, vanilla, flour, and melted butter. Mix well.

4. Stir in the pecans with the wooden spoon.

5. Put the unbaked pie shell on the cookie sheet for easy handling, pour in the filling, and bake for 30 to 35 minutes, or until the filling looks set and feels firm.

6. Wearing oven mitts, pull out the cookie sheet and remove the pie carefully to protect the pastry edge. Cool before serving.

Double-Crust Pie Pastry

This is the recipe for a pie with a top crust, such as the All-American Apple Pie (page 229). You can use it for cherry, mincemeat, or any other favorite pie filling.

Makes 1 double-crust 9-inch pie

Ingredients
2½ cups flour plus about ¼ cup for rolling out the dough
1 teaspoon salt
1 cup chilled vegetable shortening
⅓ cup (approximately) ice-cold water
1 tablespoon milk

Equipment
9-inch metal pie pan
Measuring cups
Measuring spoons
Sifter
Large mixing bowl
Pastry blender
Fork
Pastry board
Rolling pin
Small bowl
Pastry brush
Scissors
Cookie sheet
Oven mitts

1. Preheat the oven to 450°F.

2. Sift the 2½ cups of flour and the salt into the large mixing bowl and add the chilled vegetable shortening.

3. Using the pastry blender, cut the shortening into the flour until it looks like grains of rice.

4. Pour the ice water over the dough and toss it lightly with a fork until blended and you can shape it into a ball. If it is still crumbly, mix in another tablespoon or two of ice water and form into a compact ball.

5. Lay the pastry board on the counter and dust it with flour. Cut the ball of dough in half, and set one half aside. Put the other half in the center of the floured board, sprinkle a little flour on it, and pat it into a 4-inch circle.

6. Place the rolling pin across the middle of the dough and roll it out in continuous strokes, lifting the rolling pin as you get to the edge. Work your way around the dough in the same way, always starting with the rolling pin across the middle and raising it near the edge. If the dough gets a little sticky, sprinkle a little more flour on it. When you have rolled the dough out in every direction, you should have a rough circle about 14 inches in diameter. If it is appreciably smaller, repeat the rolling process with a light touch.

7. To transfer the dough to the pie plate, lay the rolling pin across the center of the finished circle, and fold the bottom half of dough up and over it. Hold the rolling pin with the draped dough over the pie plate, and unroll the dough into it, gently fitting it into the bottom and up the sides without stretching it. Don't worry about the excess dough hanging over the edge of the pie plate.

8. Fill the pie with your prepared pie filling.

9. For the top crust lay the other ball of dough on the floured pastry board and roll it out just as you did for the bottom crust, but this time roll it out to a circle only 11 inches in diameter.

10. Pour the milk into a small bowl and, using the pastry brush, paint just the edge of the lower crust that sits on the rim of the pie plate, not the overhanging dough.

11. To cover the pie filling with the top crust, use the rolling pin to transfer the dough from the pastry board as you did before, letting it fall over the filling without stretching it.

12. Leave about a 1-inch rim of dough hanging over the edge of the pie plate and cut off the excess from the bottom and top crusts with the scissors. Fold under the overhanging dough around the rim of the plate (it will be four layers thick), and seal the edges of the dough together by lightly pressing them with a fork.

13. Prick the top crust with a fork in several places to vent the steam.

14. Dip a pastry brush into the remaining milk and paint the top crust.

15. Set the pie on the cookie sheet, for easy handling, and bake it for 10 minutes, then lower the oven heat to 350°F. and bake for another 30 to 40 minutes, or until the top is lightly browned.

16. With oven mitts on, remove the cookie sheet with the pie from the oven. Take the pie off the cookie sheet, being careful to protect the pie edge, and let it cool.

All-American Apple Pie

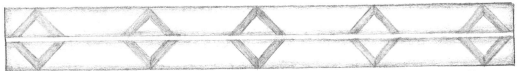

One of the nice things about this pie is that it's in season all year round. Serve it with ice cream or Cheddar cheese.

Makes 1 double-crust 9-inch pie

Ingredients
½ cup granulated sugar
½ cup light brown sugar
1 teaspoon ground cinnamon
3 pounds (about 5) tart cooking apples, such as Greenings or Granny Smiths
1 Double-Crust Pie Pastry (page 226)
1½ tablespoons butter

Equipment
Measuring cups
Measuring spoons
Large mixing bowl
Paring knife
Large spoon
Oven mitts

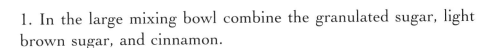

1. In the large mixing bowl combine the granulated sugar, light brown sugar, and cinnamon.

2. Cut each apple into quarters, then peel and core each quarter. Cut each quarter in half lengthwise, then make 4 crosswise cuts so you get 8 pieces per quarter. As you cut the apples, drop the pieces into the sugar mixture. When you have prepared all the apples, toss them gently with a large spoon until they are well coated. Set them aside.

3. Preheat the oven to 450°F.

4. Make the pastry and line the baking pan with the bottom crust, following the recipe for the Double-Crust Pie Pastry.

5. Spoon the sugared apples into the pie pan and spread them evenly around the bottom. Cut the butter into bits with the paring knife and dot them over the apples.

6. Still following the recipe for the Double-Crust Pie Pastry, finish the pie as directed — that is, roll out the top crust, lay it over the apples, trim the top dough, seal the edges, prick the top crust with a fork in several places, and paint the top with milk.

7. Set the pie on the cookie sheet and bake it for 10 minutes, then lower the heat and bake the pie for another 40 minutes, or until the top is browned and the apples are tender when tested with a knife.

8. Remove the cookie sheet with the pie from the oven, wearing the oven mitts, and then remove the pie carefully from the sheet.

Cookies

Brownies

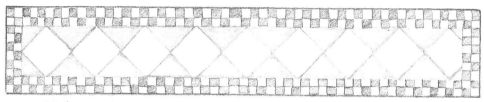

Makes 16 brownies

Ingredients

For preparing the pan:

1 to 2 teaspoons butter

1 tablespoon flour

For the brownies:

2 ounces (squares)
    unsweetened chocolate

4 tablespoons (½ stick)
    butter

1 cup sugar

2 eggs

½ cup flour

⅛ teaspoon salt

1 teaspoon vanilla

½ cup chopped walnuts

Equipment

8-inch-square pan

Measuring cup

Measuring spoons

Double boiler

Wooden spoon

Rubber spatula

Oven mitts

Cake tester

1. Preheat the oven to 325°F. Butter and flour the sides and bottom of the 8-inch-square pan.

2. Melt the chocolate in the top of the double boiler over hot but not boiling water, then remove the double boiler top and use it as a mixing bowl.

3. Add the butter, one tablespoon at a time, and stir with the wooden spoon until it is melted.

4. Gradually add the sugar, a little at a time, and stir well after each addition. Add the eggs, one at a time, and stir after each addition. Stir in half the flour until combined, then stir in the remaining flour, salt, vanilla, and nuts.

5. Spread the batter evenly in the prepared pan with the rubber spatula. Scrape the double boiler top with the spatula to get all the batter.

6. Bake for about 30 minutes, or until the top is springy and the cake tester inserted in the center comes out almost dry. Remove from the oven, wearing the oven mitts.

7. Let the brownies cool for about 10 minutes, then cut them in squares.

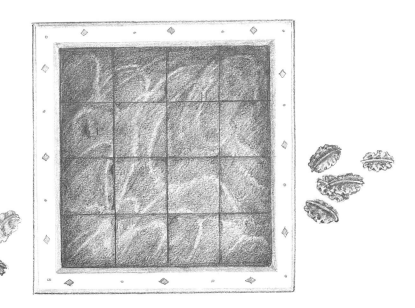

Butterscotch Brownies

These are chewy and nutty, like traditional brownies, but with a butterscotch taste.

Makes 25 squares

Ingredients

For preparing the pan:
1 to 2 teaspoons butter
1 tablespoon flour
For the brownies:
5 tablespoons butter
1 cup dark brown sugar
1 egg
¾ cup flour
1 teaspoon baking powder
¼ teaspoon salt
½ teaspoon vanilla
½ cup chopped walnuts

Equipment

8-inch-square pan
Measuring cups
Measuring spoons
Large heavy saucepan
Wooden spoon
Rubber spatula
Oven mitts
Cake tester

1. Preheat the oven to 325°F. Butter and flour the sides and bottom of the 8-inch-square pan.

2. In the heavy saucepan melt the butter over low heat, then remove pan from the heat and use it as a mixing bowl.

3. With a wooden spoon stir in the brown sugar until well com-

bined. Stir in the egg. Beat in the flour, ¼ cup at a time. Stir in the baking powder, salt, vanilla, and walnuts, and mix well together.

4. With a rubber spatula spread the batter evenly in the prepared pan, scraping out all the batter with the spatula.

5. Bake for 30 minutes, or until the top is dry and the cake tester inserted in the middle comes out clean. Remove the pan from the oven, wearing the oven mitts.

6. Let the brownies cool about 10 minutes, then cut them into squares.

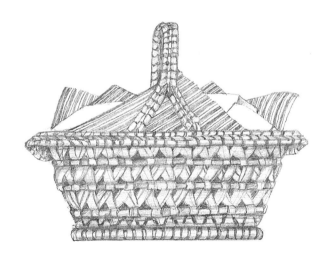

Chocolate Chip Cookies

This version of practically everyone's favorite cookie has nuts. The centers should be chewy and the edges slightly crisp.

Makes about 36 cookies

Ingredients

For preparing the cookie sheets:
1 tablespoon butter
For the cookies:
8 tablespoons (1 stick)
    butter, softened
½ cup dark brown sugar
½ cup granulated sugar
1 egg
½ teaspoon vanilla
1⅛ cups flour
½ teaspoon baking soda
½ cup chopped walnuts
1 6-ounce bag semisweet
    chocolate bits

Equipment

2 cookie sheets
Measuring cups
Measuring spoons
Electric mixer and bowl
Small mixing bowl
Wooden spoon
Teaspoon
Oven mitts
Metal spatula
Cake rack

1. Preheat the oven to 350°F. Butter the cookie sheets.

2. With the electric mixer cream the butter until it is fluffy, then gradually add the brown and white sugars, beating until the mixture is light and smooth.

3. Beat in the egg and the vanilla.

4. In the small mixing bowl combine the flour and baking soda. With the electric mixer set at medium speed, gradually add these dry ingredients to the butter-sugar mixture, blending well.

5. Stir in the nuts and chocolate bits.

6. Drop heaping teaspoonfuls of the dough onto the prepared cookie sheets about 2 inches apart, and bake about 10 to 12 minutes, or until the tops are lightly browned.

7. Wearing oven mitts, take the cookie sheets out of the oven. Remove the cookies from the sheets with the metal spatula and set them on the cake rack to cool.

8. Butter the cookie sheets again and bake the rest of the dough the same way.

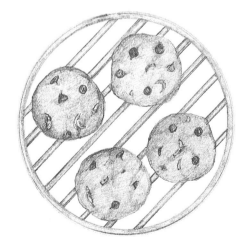

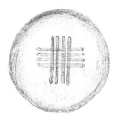

Peanut Butter Cookies

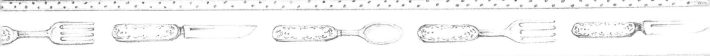

Makes about 30 cookies

Ingredients

For preparing the cookie sheets:
1 tablespoon butter
For the cookies:
1¼ cups flour plus ¼ cup
¼ teaspoon salt
½ teaspoon baking soda
8 tablespoons (1 stick)
    butter, softened
½ cup brown sugar
½ cup granulated sugar
1 egg
½ teaspoon vanilla
½ cup crunchy peanut
    butter, at room
    temperature

Equipment

2 cookie sheets
Measuring cups
Measuring spoons
Small mixing bowl
Electric mixer and bowl
Fork
Oven mitts
Metal spatula
Cake rack

1. Preheat the oven to 350°F. Butter the cookie sheets.

2. In the small mixing bowl combine 1¼ cups of the flour with the salt and baking soda and set aside.

3. With the electric mixer cream the butter until it is fluffy, then

gradually add the brown and white sugars, beating until the mixture is light and smooth.

4. Bet in the egg and the vanilla.

5. Stir in the peanut butter and the flour mixture, blending well. The dough should be stiff enough to hold its shape on a spoon; if it's too soft, stir in as much of the remaining ¼ cup flour as you need.

6. With your hands take small bits of the dough and form them into small balls. Place them about 2 inches apart on the cookie sheets. Flatten each cookie slightly and press with the back of a fork to make a striped pattern on it.

7. Bake about 8 to 10 minutes, or until the cookies feel firm to the touch.

8. Wearing the oven mitts, take the cookie sheets out of the oven. Slide the cookies from the sheets with the spatula and set them on the cake rack to cool.

9. Butter the cookie sheets again and bake the rest of the dough the same way.

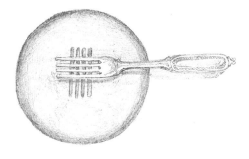

Spiced Molasses Cookies

Makes about 48 cookies

Ingredients

For preparing the cookie sheets:
1 tablespoon butter
For the cookies:
2 cups flour plus 1 to 2
    tablespoons
1 teaspoon baking soda
½ teaspoon salt
½ teaspoon ginger
½ teaspoon cinnamon
8 tablespoons (1 stick)
    butter, softened
⅓ cup brown sugar
1 egg
½ cup molasses
¼ cup milk

Equipment

2 cookie sheets
Measuring cups
Measuring spoons
Medium mixing bowl
Electric mixer and bowl
Teaspoon
Rubber spatula
Oven mitts
Metal spatula
Cake rack

1. Preheat the oven to 375°F. Butter the cookie sheets.

2. In the medium mixing bowl combine 2 cups of flour with the baking soda, salt, ginger, and cinnamon and set aside.

3. With the electric mixer cream the butter until it is fluffy, then beat in the sugar, egg, and molasses.

4. Add half the dry ingredients to the creamed mixture, and mix together at low speed. Add the milk and the remaining dry ingredients, mixing at low speed. The mixture should be just stiff enough to hold its shape when you take a spoonful. If it is softer, stir in a little more flour, a tablespoon at a time.

5. Using a teaspoon, drop spoonfuls of the batter on the cookie sheets about two inches apart. Use a rubber spatula or a finger to get the sticky dough off the spoon.

6. Bake the cookies for about 8 to 10 minutes, or until they are brown around the edges.

7. Wearing oven mitts, remove the cookie sheets from the oven. With the metal spatula, transfer the cookies to the cake rack to cool.

8. Butter the cookie sheets again and bake the rest of the dough the same way.

Oatmeal Cookies

These cookies are thin, chewy, and full of raisins.

Makes about 48 cookies

Ingredients

For preparing the cookie sheets:
1 tablespoon butter
For the cookies:
1½ cups flour
½ teaspoon baking soda
½ teaspoon salt
1 teaspoon cinnamon
1 cup (2 sticks) butter,
    softened
1 cup sugar
1 egg
1 tablespoon molasses
¼ cup milk
1¾ cup regular oatmeal,
    uncooked
1 cup raisins

Equipment

2 cookie sheets
Measuring cups
Measuring spoons
Medium mixing bowl
Electric mixer and bowl
Wooden spoon
Soup spoon
Oven mitts
Metal spatula
Cake rack

1. Preheat the oven to 325°F. and butter the cookie sheets.

2. In the medium mixing bowl combine the flour with the baking soda, salt, and cinnamon and set aside.

3. With the electric mixer cream the butter until it is fluffy, then beat in the sugar, egg, and molasses.

4. Add the dry ingredients to the creamed mixture, and mix them together at low speed. Add the milk and the oatmeal, mixing at low speed.

5. Stir in the raisins with the wooden spoon.

6. Using the soup spoon, drop spoonfuls of the batter on the prepared cookie sheets about 1½ to 2 inches apart.

7. Bake the cookies for about 10 to 12 minutes, or until they are brown around the edges.

8. Wearing oven mitts, remove the cookie sheets from the oven. With the spatula, transfer the cookies to the cake rack to cool.

9. Butter the cookie sheets again and bake the rest of the dough the same way.

Raisin Nut Cookies

These are slightly chewy cookies with a hint of cinnamon, full of raisins and nuts.

Makes 36 cookies

Ingredients

For preparing the cookie sheets:
1 tablespoon butter
For the cookies:
1 cup flour
¼ teaspoon baking soda
⅛ teaspoon salt
½ teaspoon ground
        cinnamon
5 tablespoons butter,
        softened
½ cup sugar
1 egg
⅓ cup chopped walnuts
⅓ cup raisins

Equipment

2 cookie sheets
Measuring cups
Measuring spoons
Medium mixing bowl
Electric mixer and bowl
Wooden spoon
Teaspoon
Oven mitts
Metal spatula
Cake rack

1. Preheat the oven to 350°F. and butter the cookie sheets.

2. In the medium mixing bowl combine the flour, baking soda, salt, and cinnamon and set aside.

244

3. With the electric mixer cream the butter until it is fluffy, then beat in the sugar and the egg.

4. Add the dry ingredients to the creamed mixture and mix them together at low speed. Stir in the nuts and raisins with the wooden spoon.

5. Using the teaspoon, drop spoonfuls of the batter on the prepared cookie sheets about 1½ to 2 inches apart.

6. Bake the cookies for about 10 minutes, or until they are brown around the edges.

7. Wearing oven mitts, remove the cookie sheets from the oven. With the spatula, transfer the cookies to the cake rack to cool.

8. Butter the cookie sheets again and bake the rest of the dough the same way.

Meringues

Meringues are melt-in-your-mouth sweets. Large shells are wonderful filled with ice cream and topped with crushed fruit or a sauce. Small ones are perfect party cookies. They keep a long time, so you can make them days before you need them.

Makes 8 to 12 shells or up to 40 small cookies

Ingredients	Equipment
2 egg whites, at room temperature	2 cookie sheets
	Scissors
½ cup (8 tablespoons) superfine sugar	Parchment or brown paper
	Measuring cups
½ teaspoon vanilla	Measuring spoons
⅛ teaspoon salt	Electric mixer and bowl
½ cup chopped walnuts (optional)	Rubber spatula
	Large spoon or teaspoon

1. Preheat the oven to 225°F. Cut parchment paper or brown paper to fit on the 2 cookie sheets.

2. With the electric mixer beat the egg whites until they are stiff but not dry and stand up in straight peaks when you lift out the beater.

3. Slowly beat in 6 tablespoons of the sugar, a tablespoon at a

time, beating well after each addition. Beat in the vanilla and the salt.

4. With the rubber spatula, not the mixer, fold in the remaining 2 tablespoons of sugar, and the chopped nuts, if you are using them.

5. For meringue shells use the large spoon to heap the egg whites on the prepared cookie sheets, shaping them into rough shells about 3 inches in diameter with a center depression. For small meringue cookies, drop the egg whites by teaspoonfuls on the prepared cookie sheets. Either way, place the meringues about an inch apart.

6. Bake the meringues for 1 hour. Turn off the heat and, without opening the oven door, leave them in the oven several more hours or overnight. They must dry thoroughly to be crisp.

7. When they are cool and dry, remove from the cookie sheets and store in an airtight container until you are ready to use them.

More Desserts

Denver Chocolate Pudding

This is a triple-treat dessert — a crusty top, a cakelike pudding in the center, and a thick chocolate sauce on the bottom.

Serves 6

Ingredients

For preparing the baking dish:
1 tablespoon butter
For the pudding:
2 tablespoons butter
1 ounce (square)
    unsweetened chocolate
¾ cup granulated sugar
1 cup flour
2 teaspoons baking powder
⅛ teaspoon salt
½ cup milk
1 teaspoon vanilla
For the topping:
½ cup light brown sugar
½ cup granulated sugar
4 tablespoons unsweetened
    cocoa
1 cup cold water

Equipment

8-inch-round by 3-inch-high
    baking or soufflé dish
Measuring cups
Measuring spoons
Heavy saucepan
Large mixing bowl
Wooden spoon
Small bowl
Large spoon
Oven mitts

1. Preheat the oven to 325°F. and butter the baking dish.

2. In the heavy saucepan melt the butter and the chocolate. Remove from the heat and let cool slightly.

3. In the large mixing bowl combine the sugar, flour, baking powder, and salt. With the wooden spoon stir in the chocolate mixture, then add the milk and vanilla, and stir until well blended. It will be lumpy.

4. Pour the mixture into the prepared baking dish, and set aside.

5. In the small bowl combine the light brown sugar, granulated sugar, and cocoa for the topping with the large spoon. Spoon the topping over the pudding in the baking dish and pour the cold water over the top.

6. Bake the pudding about 45 to 50 minutes, or until it looks set. Wearing the oven mitts, remove the pudding from the oven. Let it stand at room temperature and serve it cool.

Fresh Fruit Mélange

Fresh fruit in season is a wonderful dessert, and some fruits go particularly well together — grapefruit and orange sections; orange and banana slices sprinkled with coconut flakes; fresh pineapple cubes and strawberries; watermelon, cantaloupe, and honeydew melon balls; nectarines, peaches, and blueberries.

½ cup per serving

1. Cut your favorite fruits into neat pieces, combine in a large bowl, cover, and chill. If you are using any berries, add them just before serving.

2. Taste and stir in a little sugar or lemon juice, if you like. Then pile into sherbet glasses and garnish with sprigs of mint leaves.

Marinated Oranges

This is a year-round treat, easy to make, and refreshing.

Makes 6 servings

Ingredients
3 navel oranges
¼ cup Seville orange
   marmalade (with slivers
   of rind)
¼ cup orange juice

Equipment
Measuring cups
Sharp knife
Cutting board
Large serving bowl
Small bowl
Whisk
Large spoon
Plastic wrap

1. Peel the oranges with the sharp knife, starting at the top and cutting around and around in a spiral to remove the rind and as much of the white pith under it as possible. Remove any remaining white sections. Slice the oranges crosswise about ¼ inch thick on the cutting board and put them in the serving bowl.

2. In the small bowl combine the orange marmalade and orange juice with a whisk. Spoon the mixture over the orange slices to

coat them well. Cover the orange slices with plastic wrap and chill them in the refrigerator.

3. When you are ready to serve the oranges, spoon the juice mixture over the slices again.

Baked Apples

This version of baked apples has raisins and spices. Serve them warm or cold, with cream, if you like, or a dollop of ice cream.

Serves 4

Ingredients
4 baking apples, such as
    Granny Smiths or Rome
    Beauties
4 tablespoons sugar
1 tablespoon cinnamon
Dash nutmeg
2 tablespoons raisins
1 cup orange juice

Equipment
Measuring spoons
Measuring cup
Apple corer
Peeling knife
Small bowl
Oven-proof glass baking dish
Large spoon or bulb baster
Cake tester
Oven mitts
Plastic wrap for the
    microwave

1. Preheat the oven to 400°F. for oven baking. Or microwave the apples (see below).

2. Wash the apples and remove the stems. Starting from the other end, core each apple about three-fourths through, discarding the core. At the cored end peel the top third of the apple.

3. In the small bowl combine the sugar, cinnamon, and nutmeg.

255

Spoon the mixture evenly into the cored apples. Stuff the raisins into the apples over the sugar mixture.

4. Set the apples in an oven-proof glass baking dish large enough so they don't touch each other and pour the orange juice in the bottom of the dish.

5. Bake for 30 minutes, basting the apples with the juices in the dish once or twice, using the spoon or bulb baster. Test for doneness with the cake tester. The apples should be soft but not falling apart. Bake longer, if necessary.

To microwave: Prepare and stuff the apples, as above. After placing them in the glass baking dish, cover them tightly with plastic wrap. Cook in the microwave on High for 5½ minutes. Remove dish from the microwave, wearing oven mitts, pierce the plastic wrap on the far side to let the steam out, and let the apples sit for 5 minutes.

Dessert Sauces

Dessert sauces are wonderful to have on hand, to top off ice cream, meringues, and plain cakes. If you have any sauce left, store it in the refrigerator; you can usually stretch a fruit sauce by adding orange juice to it, and the other sauces by stirring in a little cream.

Chocolate Sauce

This is a good sauce for many occasions, and you can serve it hot or cold.

Makes about 1½ cups

Ingredients
4 tablespoons (½ stick)
    butter
2 ounces (squares)
    unsweetened chocolate
1 cup sugar
⅛ teaspoon salt
½ cup water
1 teaspoon vanilla

Equipment
Measuring cup
Measuring spoons
Small heavy saucepan
Wooden spoon

1. Put the butter and chocolate in the saucepan over moderate heat and stir with the wooden spoon until smooth.

2. Add the sugar, salt, and water and stir over moderate heat until the sauce comes almost to a boil and thickens, about 5 minutes.

3. Remove from the heat and let cool a little, then stir in the vanilla.

Hot Fudge Sauce

This is an all-time favorite for ice cream sundaes. Store it in the refrigerator, then heat it in the top of a double boiler over hot water.

Makes about 1½ cups

Ingredients
1 tablespoon butter
2 ounces (squares)
    unsweetened chocolate
½ cup boiling water
1 cup sugar
2 tablespoons corn syrup
⅛ teaspoon salt
½ teaspoon vanilla

Equipment
Measuring cups
Measuring spoons
Heavy saucepan
Wooden spoon

1. Put the butter and chocolate in the saucepan over moderate heat and stir with the wooden spoon until melted. Add the boiling water slowly, stirring constantly.

2. Bring the mixture to a boil, then stir in the sugar, corn syrup, and salt. Cook 5 minutes over moderate heat, stirring often, then remove the saucepan from the heat. Let the mixture cool slightly, then stir in the vanilla.

Butterscotch Sauce

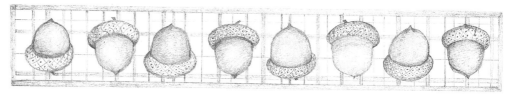

Another favorite ice cream topping. You can add a tablespoon or two of cream, or chopped nuts, if you like.

Makes about 1 cup

Ingredients
½ cup dark brown sugar
½ cup light corn syrup
2 tablespoons butter
¼ teaspoon salt
1 teaspoon vanilla

Equipment
Measuring cups
Measuring spoons
Small heavy saucepan
Wooden spoon

1. Combine the sugar and corn syrup in the saucepan and cook over low heat about 8 to 10 minutes, stirring constantly with the wooden spoon.

2. Remove from the heat and stir in the butter, salt, and vanilla.

Raspberry Sauce

This is a useful sauce that dresses up fresh peaches, chocolate fudge cakes, and, of course, ice cream.

Makes about 1¼ cups

Ingredients
2 cups raspberries, fresh or
    frozen
¼ cup superfine sugar
3 teaspoons fresh lemon juice
    (optional)

Equipment
Measuring cups
Measuring spoons
Food processor or blender
Strainer or sieve
Small heavy saucepan
Soup spoon
Wooden spoon

1. Process the berries in the food processor or blender until they are pureed.

2. Set the strainer or sieve over the saucepan, and pour in the puree. To remove the seeds press the puree through the sieve with the back of the soup spoon.

3. Stir in the sugar with the wooden spoon and cook over medium heat until the sugar is dissolved.

4. Remove from the heat and cool. If the sauce is too sweet, stir in a little lemon juice, one teaspoon at a time, to taste.

Whipped Cream

This is a topping for fresh fruit, ice cream, many cakes, and hot cocoa. If the dessert is sweet, don't add any extra sugar. Don't whip the cream more than an hour before you want to use it.

Makes 1½ to 2 cups

Ingredients
1 cup (half pint) heavy
    cream
2 teaspoons confectioners'
    sugar
1 teaspoon vanilla

Equipment
Measuring cups
Measuring spoons
Metal bowl
Rotary hand beater
Plastic wrap

1. Chill the cream, the metal bowl, and the beater in the refrigerator.

2. Whip the cream until it holds soft peaks. Beat in the sugar and vanilla, and continue beating just until the cream stands up in peaks when you lift the beaters.

3. Cover with plastic wrap and store in the refrigerator up to an hour until ready to use. Serve in a chilled bowl.

Ice Cream Variations

Ice cream is an all-time favorite dessert, and there are many ways to serve it. Put a scoop in a Meringue Shell (page 246), or in a fresh or frozen peach half, then top with a sauce.

Or make your own ice cream mix-ins. Let vanilla, chocolate, or coffee ice cream soften, then stir in one or more of the following: chopped nuts, candied ginger, crushed peppermint candy, peanut brittle, crumbled pieces of your favorite cookies or candy. Then refreeze the ice cream until ready to serve.

Drinks

Hot Cocoa

Makes 5 cups

Ingredients
⅓ cup unsweetened cocoa
¼ cup sugar
⅓ cup water
Few grains salt
4 cups milk
½ teaspoon vanilla
Whipped cream (page 262),
    optional

Equipment
Large saucepan
Measuring cups
Measuring spoons
Wire whisk

1. Combine the cocoa and sugar in the saucepan. Add the water and bring to a boil, stirring occasionally, and cook over moderate heat for 3 minutes. Add the salt.

2. Add the milk and heat slowly until the cocoa is hot but not boiling.

3. Remove from the heat, beat the cocoa with the wire whisk until frothy, and stir in the vanilla. Serve with a bowl of whipped cream, if you like.

Variations

Mexican Chocolate: Add ½ teaspoon instant coffee and ¼ teaspoon cinnamon to each cup of hot cocoa.

Holiday Cheer: Serve the hot cocoa in holiday-decorated mugs and add a small peppermint candy cane to each mug.

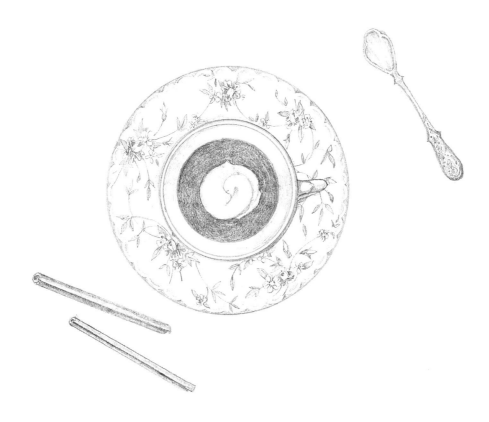

Coffee

Coffee should be freshly made, strong, and piping hot. You can buy whole coffee beans and grind them at the store or at home in your own coffee grinder. Automatic electric coffee makers brew excellent coffee.

General rules for making good coffee:

1. Keep coffee beans or ground coffee tightly covered in the refrigerator or freezer. You can use beans or ground coffee right from the freezer.

2. For hot coffee, use 2 level tablespoons of coffee for every cup of water. For iced coffee, use ¼ cup of coffee per cup of water.

3. Always use the right grind — drip grind for drip method, regular grind for percolator, fine grind for espresso (which requires a special coffee maker).

4. Keep brewed coffee fresh and hot for long periods of time in a vacuum pitcher or thermos.

5. Reheat an individual mug or cup of room-temperature coffee in a microwave on High for 1½ minutes.

6. Keep your coffee maker absolutely clean. Wash it with a mild detergent and periodically run it just with water and some baking soda. Run it again with clear water.

Tea

Boiling water is the secret to good tea. You can use loose tea or tea bags, as long as the tea steeps in boiling — not just hot — water. General rules for making good tea:

1. Store tea in a tightly covered container away from sunlight.

2. Earthenware or china teapots keep the true flavor of tea better than metal.

3. Just before brewing tea always warm the teapot or mug by rinsing it out with hot water.

4. Always brew tea with fresh boiling water. Pour it over tea leaves in a warmed teapot or mug, cover, and let steep for 4 or 5 minutes.

5. For hot tea use 1 teaspoon of loose tea or 1 tea bag for every cup of water. For iced tea use 2 teaspoons of loose tea or 2 tea bags per cup of water and set aside to cool; use more tea if you are going to pour the hot tea directly over ice cubes.

6. Serve hot tea with sugar, cream or milk, and lemon or orange slices; have a pot of hot water ready to dilute the tea. Serve iced tea over cracked ice or ice cubes in tall glasses garnished with a sprig of mint, with superfine sugar and lemon or orange slices.

Cranberry Punch

This is a great drink for a big party.

Makes 3 quarts

Ingredients
1 cup superfine sugar
1 quart hot water
1 quart cranberry juice
Juice of ½ large lemon
2 cups orange juice
1 quart sparkling water or
    ginger ale

Equipment
Large pot
Measuring cup
Punch bowl or large pitcher

1. In the large pot or pitcher dissolve the sugar in the hot water. Add the cranberry, lemon, and orange juices, and stir. Chill.

2. Just before serving, add the sparkling water or ginger ale and pour over ice in the punch bowl or large pitcher.

Lemonade

Makes about 1½ quarts

Ingredients
1 cup superfine sugar
1 cup hot water
½ cup fresh lemon juice
1 quart cold water
Mint sprigs

Equipment
Large pitcher
Measuring cups

1. In the large pitcher dissolve the sugar in the hot water and let cool.

2. Stir in the lemon juice and the cold water, add 6 to 8 ice cubes, and chill.

3. Serve in tall glasses with sprigs of mint.

Mulled Cider

This is a wonderful winter drink, especially with plain cookies or doughnuts.

Makes 1 quart

Ingredients
1 quart apple cider
½ teaspoon allspice
Three whole cloves
1 stick cinnamon, about 3
    inches long
¼ cup brown sugar

Equipment
Medium saucepan
Measuring cups
Measuring spoons

1. In the medium saucepan heat the cider with the allspice, cloves, and cinnamon and cook over moderate heat for 5 minutes. Add the sugar, bring to a boil, and cook for 5 more minutes.

2. Serve piping hot in small punch glasses.

Milk Shakes

Strictly speaking, a shake is chilled milk mixed with a flavored syrup. You can turn it into a frosted by blending in a scoop or two of ice cream.

Serves 1

Ingredients
1 cup chilled milk
2 tablespoons flavored syrup,
    such as chocolate,
    maple, coffee,
    strawberry, or
2 teaspoons vanilla
1 to 2 scoops ice cream, such
    as chocolate, coffee,
    strawberry, vanilla,
    maple (optional)

Equipment
Blender or food processor
Measuring cup
Measuring spoons
Ice cream scoop (optional)

1. Spin all ingredients together in the blender or food processor.

Ice Cream Sodas

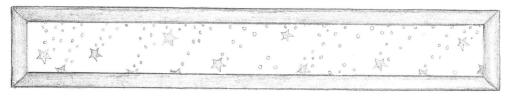

Serves 1

Ingredients
3 tablespoons flavored syrup,
    such as chocolate,
    coffee, strawberry, or
    fruit-flavored jam
1 cup sparkling water
1 to 2 scoops ice cream

Equipment
Measuring cup
Measuring spoons
Long-handled spoon

1. Put the syrup in a tall glass, add a splash of the sparkling water, and stir well. Add the ice cream. Fill with sparkling water and stir well. Serve with a long-handled spoon and a straw.

Index